Ready to Sling
SuperFood
SuperHero Eats?
cape optional...

"The more you Praise and Celebrate your Life, the more there is in Life to Celebrate." - Oprah Winfrey

"The Triple Berry Acai JingLato was the most amazing experience of my life. I have never eaten food that tastes so good, and that has the quality of and the immediate impact of a high-powered supplement. It was outrageous! I've never experienced the complexity and the blending of flavors, spices and herbs in my life, I am humbled by your mastery."

-Catherine Oxenberg, Actor, Director, Founder Body of Bliss

"The JingSlingers have successfully created a unique, signature flavor profile that can only be described as transcendent and revelatory. From sweet to savory foods, tonics, and elixirs - they are masters of creating healthy, familiar comfort food recipes that you can't believe are actually good for you! They infuse all of their creations with passion, heart, intention and boundless creativity. I always leave their table feeling elevated, elated and totally connected to my inner child.

"Food With Benefits" is the ultimate culmination of their wellness wisdom, world-class culinary prowess and collective ethos to heal the world. This book is a powerful tool to create more joy, health, happiness and satisfaction in your life!"

- Jason Wrobel, Celebrity Vegan Chef, Author & host of "How to Live to 100" on Cooking Channel

"This is no cookbook, this is a masterpiece of culinary alchemy! With every bite and every sip your body will transform, your mind will awaken and your life will be changed forever.
Joy and Jay have just JingSmacked your taste buds with love!"

- Dr. George Lamoureux, Founder & CEO, Jing Herbs

'I had the privilege of tasting some of Joy and Jay's SuperFood creations when they were on my radio show. The desserts they brought tasted fantastic and there was no "sugar crash" afterward. **The board operators at the station went crazy over them!** The JingSlingers do a great service by combining SuperFoods, loaded with nutrients that taste great! What a concept - good tasting food that is actually good for you! Thanks for sharing these recipes with the rest of us and keep up the tremendous work!'

-Jay D. Foster, Body Chemistry Nutritional Biochemist, Miami, FL

"Enjoying food with Joy and Jay is an experience unlike any other culinary treat I have ever had. The love and care they pour into their creations is palpable. What they are able to do without sugar is nothing short of miraculous. Flavor and beauty is always present. What always stays with me is the Love I feel from the nourishment they provide."

- Ele Keats, Actor, Founder, Ele Keats Jewelry

Thank you for the food before us,

the friends beside us and

the Love between us.

2015
Collector's Edition
Number

of 5,000 printed with
100% Green
Materials

Food With Benefits copyright
© 2015 JingSlingers Inc,
Joy Coelho & Jay Denman

Photography by Jeff Skeirik, Rawtographer
Additional photography by
Joy Coelho & Jay Denman

ISBN: 978-0-9964668-4-4
Library of Congress Control Number: 2015914805

Written, illustrated and designed
by Joy Coelho & Jay Denman
some images by ShutterStock

Contact WaterStone Media for wholesale, special or corporate
bulk orders at JingSlingers@gmail.com

Food With Benefits

Gluten-Free, Sugar-Free SuperFood Recipes
Paleo, Vegan & Omnivore Clever Comfort Foods

Joy Coelho & Jay Denman

Foreward by Bestselling Author Tess Masters

Contents

Dedication

For JingMaster Truth Calkins, who was the center of the original Tonic Bar Vortex in Los Angeles for a decade, and whose inspiration continues to reverberate out into the cosmos exponentially.

We love you Brother, Joy & Jay

One of the many gifts that my parents, *John & Joanne Coelho*, blessed us with was creating wonderful food with great love and imagination. Every birthday, beach picnic and packed lunch held the message that we were *so loved*.

This book is a celebration of the wit, wisdom and love passed down to all six of us and now to their grandchildren around each and every one of our dinner tables. *Momma, you inspire me beyond words, this book is dedicated to you -*

All My Love Always, Joy

For my parents, Nancy and Jim Denman. Thank you for your unconditional love and for always supporting me in following my dharma, wherever it has led me.

You are shining examples that with awareness and a bit-by-bit approach, anyone, no matter their age, can start to improve their diet and their health this very day, and that "growing older" can actually mean feeling and looking better each year because you are slowing down and even reversing facets of the "aging process."

"Saging" instead of "aging" is the philosophy, not only physically, but even more importantly, mentally becoming more adaptogenic and wise with every passing year. You both exemplify this principle and I couldn't be more proud.

Love You! Jay

A Sweet Word From Steven Tyler

- Aerosmith Lead Singer, Grammy Award Winning Artist & Rock Music Legend

"The JingSlingers... how can I express my relationship with them and their food? Maybe it's like this... ¡ ¡ ¡ ¡ ¡

I used to love the candy NERDS... but I stopped eating them when I realized that for me it was basically cannibalism. I guess the point here is that their food is fun to eat!

When I'm done with one of their meals and I'm satiated beyond belief... and I top it off with one of Joy's Bliss Brownies or her Coconut Crème Brûlée... I'm always floored to find out that what I just devoured was dairy-free, gluten-free, SUGAR-FREE and has more vitamins, minerals and nutrients than an 8 course meal served by Mother Nature herself. Totally satisfied without feeling full.

Do yourself a glorious *flavor* and commit to enriching your mind, body, and soul with Joy and Jay's life-changing recipe gems!

Remember... you are only as young as the last time you changed your mind!"

8

Foreward

The JingSlingers and their culinary wellness philosophy changed my life.

Are you ready to enjoy food that blows your mind and taste buds sky high, while boosting your health into the stratosphere? Then Joy and Jay are ready, willing, and able to change your life, too.

What you're holding in your hands should not be confused with yet one more collection of healthy recipes. You're about to experience what can happen when next-level nutrition finds itself in the hands of culinary geniuses who are also wellness maestros. Joy and Jay harmonize encyclopedic knowledge of the power of superfoods, herbs and tinctures with brilliant flair for pairing flavors and textures. You and I reap the reward: exquisite functional food that heals, balances, and nourishes in ways surpassing the imagination. Until now.

The benefits of this food run the gamut. Some recipes get me supercharged, energized, and feeling like I'm firing on all cylinders for the first time in my life. Ready to take on the world, or go out and save it. Some recipes take me the other way, with dishes that leave me calmed, balanced, and grounded, helping me to get a sound sleep and wake up deeply rested and recharged. Whatever you're after - hormone balance, heightened mental clarity, an antioxidant blast, or anything else on the wellness spectrum - you'll find foods here that deliver it.

And the best part: The food is fun! The JingSlingers take the funk of out of functional food. Reinventing healthy food as comfort food, Joy and Jay have worked up gluten-free, sugar-free, super-boosted versions of classic drinks, salads, breads, ice creams, doughnuts, cookies, cakes, and pies - all of which blow their conventional counterparts right out of the water.

I've been lucky enough to be on hand with other people - hundreds, in fact - when they experience this food revelation. Their reactions are always a thrill and send me into nostalgia for my own first time: "Wow! *Un-buh-leev-able*! What's in it? This actually *heals* my body?!"

These recipes go way beyond merely shattering conventional expectations of what's possible with flavor and nutrition. I could go on and on, but I'll let the food do the talking. The proof is truly in the JingSlingers' pudding.

Make the recipes. No matter what your health goals or your dietary preferences, this food will rock your world. And it won't be just a JingSling fling - it'll be a lifelong love affair.

This book is a game changer. Game on! *Tess Masters*

Tess Masters, Bestselling Author of *The Blender Girl*
and *The Blender Girl Smoothies*

Introduction

Why We Sling...

This book is intended to inspire you on many different levels.

First, you are now armed with *Comfort Food Recipes* that you, along with your friends and family, can enjoy no matter what kind of diet or food preferences you desire. Paleo, Vegan, Vegetarian, and everyday Omnivores will be floored when they can finally all sit down to *Nutrient Dense* Wraps, Pizza, Chili, Ice Cream, Soups and so much more. This is thanks to the culinary wizardry of infusing SuperFoods, SuperHerbs and Powerful Powders while swapping out the unhealthy conventional stand-ins for our SuperHero upgrades.

These recipes have been cleverly tuned-up to meet a variety of healthy culinary requests by showing you how to *Sling* them organic, gluten-free, grain-free, dairy-free, soy-free or processed sugar-free, or whatever your preference may be. These are clean, body rejuvenating recipes where our "Everyone is Welcome at Our Table," philosophy can reboot your dinnertime for the better.

Secondly, we wish to inspire the instinctual cook in you. Eating with the seasons, bypassing industrial preservatives for fresh ingredients and produce, making that pie or bread that your Grandma use to make, and therefore conjuring warm memories while passing a precious healthy tradition down to your kids is our intention.

Next, you are going to get an unexpected education about your **new eats** based in cutting-edge science that is in concert with ancient wisdom. All of which are supported by research and a JingNami of endnotes.

This is where you will realize we are nutritional biochemistry science geeks with biohacking chops that work in sync with our unique culinary backgrounds. Hence, our official title - ***JingMaster Alchemical Culinary Artisans***. We want you to understand that by honoring your true primal blueprint, you can bring about an upgraded level of wellness made possible by a dessert or side dish that looks normal but tastes sensational.

Here is the bonus, the Crème Brûlée you are enjoying can now be both fat-burning and beautifying... Wait... What?! Yep, it is all here and now you can devour it page by page, pick your favorites, *Sling* them one-by-one and impress your biggest foodie friends forever.

Last but not least, it is your birthright to know how to Sling simple remedies and immunity boosters from the heart of your home, your kitchen. Soups, Drinks, Elixirs and Shots that help to get your body back on track quickly with real food and real nutrition are what's on the menu. A lot of the passed-down-through-generations remedies or wives' tales that your parents and grandparents used were scientifically spot on and now have been proven with modern research.

We wish for you to learn to fully embrace this *"Nourish to Flourish"* sensibility, especially if it means making your pizza from scratch instead of ordering from the closest joint that delivers.

Feed all of your senses and enjoy what ***feel good food*** can do for you!

Joy's Story

I grew up in the kitchen and there was always plenty to learn. my Mom was a professional baker and made magic for her six kids every time she picked up her measuring cups. I would stand up on the big white wooden chair to reach the counter top just to have my little fingers in the sweet bread dough or to help crack walnuts and peel potatoes.

There were always three extra candles on every one of our homemade birthday cakes. Momma told us these were special candles signifying "Health, Wealth & Happiness" and any wish that we made as we blew out the flames, would be granted along with these additional blessings.

Health and happiness WAS the wealth being infused into me at every meal back then. I had no idea how fortunate I was at the time, growing up with home cooked meals and treats made from scratch wasn't the norm for my friends even back then. I remember fussing about having to eat the fresh fish my Dad had caught the night before, because I wanted "normal fish sticks" like the ones I saw in the school cafeteria. Our fruits and vegetables came from the local Farmer's Market and the meat from the butcher shop.
This was different than the popular "TV dinners" in aluminum trays being served in our neighbors' homes.

Our home was always filled with the glorious scents of morning pancakes, baking bread, Toll House cookies and brownies in the afternoon and then savory dinners like Portuguese Kale Soup and Paella.
Our family's Fall favorite... *Cue the singing angels...* Pumpkin Pie!

Now then... I can cook, grill, sous vide, bake, Sling, blend and create awesome, crave-worthy "just about any dish you throw-down eats," BUT... I am still one half note short of how awesome my Mom's Pumpkin Pie is at every holiday dinner.

She has a "Je ne sais quoi" in her touch that I am a mere dalton away from executing. I finally understand it is her vibrational signature of love infused into that perfect crust and pumpkin custard filling that makes it those perfect flavors sing.

Living on my own in my twenties, pizza delivery, fast food and dinners packaged in plastic pouches and pods became my food source along with my first microwave... Not a good combo.

I was in good physical condition, my career as a Police Officer demanded it. My weekly Police Canine Handler and S.W.A.T. team training required strength and agility. Even though I was working out and training weekly, the shift to "convenient food" and zap frying it all in the microwave was stealing my energy a little shave at a time. I chalked up the re-occurring joint pain and restless sleep to turning thirty and working the night shift. I had overcome a broken back and temporary paralysis from an all-terrain vehicle accident. Coming back from not being able to walk was humbling and being 100% again was a blessing I attribute to having a strong constitution and refusing the surgery to insert metal rods and screws in my spine. That decision was purely instinctual as I didn't know then what I know now.

When it came to food, like most people, I was completely clueless that I was sacrificing my health and longevity for convenience. Eating out was certainly easier than making my own lunch or dinner... but I was about to find out the hard way how important it was to eat real, uncorrupted food like I had done as a child.

My body was trying to juggle the undetected pesticides, chemicals and toxins at hyperspeed just to catch up and then it began archiving those nasties in my fat. This biochemical tango was overwhelming my body's natural homeostasis, unbeknownst to me at the time.

The sleeplessness was a screaming red flag indicating a lack of essential nutrients. The pain and swelling of my joints was a warning that my unwittingly self-induced inflammation from rancid and/or GMO oils, not to mention the other countless chemical additives, were now hijacking my meatsuit and aging me prematurely.

The altered gluten and chemical stabilizers in conventional grocery store bread, crackers and cookies gave me a bloated gastric nightmare, while a particular nightshade (conventional potatoes) stole my energy.

Over-the-counter antacids, aspirin, acetaminophen and sleep aids were recommended by my doctor and so that is what I did. "This is what happens when you get older," he said to me as he swallowed two pills and washed them down with a diet soda for his chronic headaches. "But you can manage it with these OTCs." This was his parting advice. I was never asked, by any physician, about my diet.

In my late forties it finally took a medical "two-by-four" to change my level of awareness. This DEFCON 1 health crisis was a blessing in disguise as it changed my wellness trajectory for the better... and for good.

"Like most people, I was completely clueless that I was sacrificing my Health and Longevity for Convenience."

15

I was still on the conventional medical train after rounds of fertility shots, more injections and synthetic pills for endometriosis, and with all of this I found myself more than 100 pounds overweight. I then switched to low-fat or no-fat dairy and consumed soy everything: milk, cheese, protein, ice cream and baked goods. I dumped real butter for canola oil margarine, thinking it was better. A synthetic lab created sweetener became my sugar of choice. Little did I know about its neurotoxicity and that I had, over time, created the perfect storm for an urgent trip to the surgical suite resulting in a full hysterectomy, removal of a tumor the size of a grapefruit and instant overnight menopause.

At my post surgery check up I was handed a fist full of prescriptions for high blood pressure, high blood sugar, high cholesterol, migraines, GERD and insomnia along with the standard synthetic hormone replacement protocol covered by my insurance. Red flags were flying... I never picked up those medications, I chose to learn everything I could to heal and rejuvenate myself with nature. That was more than 10 years ago.

While I was still in the hospital recovering from that surgery, I began spending pretty much every waking moment researching, investigating, and immersing myself in nutritional education with the cutting edge Doctors, Nutritional Biochemists and renowned Longevity Experts in how to have "Blue Zone" SuperHero health. Thousands of hours of education, mentorship and hands-on experience allowed me to see not only how I got myself into that mess, but most importantly, how to reverse and mitigate the damage I had done.

" You can heal and rejuvenate far and away faster and better than you have ever been told or lead to believe, this I know is true.

Becoming a Green Consultant, a Tonic Chinese Herbalist and a SuperFood Specialist elevated my life, my health and my culinary skills to a whole other level. It gave me a broader view how my every day choices navigate my wellness journey and destination.

I wanted the food that we all love, to love us back. Through those years I was scientifically sifting out the most sound principles from the Whole Food & Raw Movement, Body Ecology Diet, Primal Diet, Macrobiotics, the Genotype & Blood Type Diets, absorbed the multifaceted benefits of Organic Flora & Fauna, learned Chinese and Ayurvedic schools of thought and now the upgrades that the Bulletproof Diet and its science provides. I have found a multitude of answers for anti-aging and thriving with nature through these principles using specific Supplements, SuperFoods and SuperHerbs with mindful application.

Creating functional food that has been transformed into Clever Comfort Food has become my art. Mastering the alchemy, the mouth feel and the flavors is what has made our celebrity clients love what we can do for their health, beauty, longevity, daily performance and... Oh yes, their taste buds.

When I am asked, "What do you do?" My answer is "I am a JingMaster Alchemical Culinary Artisan... basically a SuperFood SuperHero, I create Clever Comfort Food that is anti-aging, fat-burning, promotes mental clarity, sound sleep and natural energy." Then they eat the JingLato, drink the Margarita, gobble up our Charmed Chili and the nutrient density hits them. Some sensitive folks feel the powerful affects right away, other people sleep great that night, feel a bump in their energy or note a clarity in their brain and that's when we get the excited texts or phone calls. Yes, you have been "Slung!"

My Police background automatically compels me to get the whole story, not just a cherry-picked fraction to validate a certain point of view from any one source. It is why our philosophy is grounded in "Everyone is Welcome at Our Table." The key here is to know your meatsuit, really know your biochemistry, constitution, and genotype. We have resources for you so you too can find out how you tick. Overlaying this information with the right foods to match your *season in life* can help you turn the corner and bring about wellness you no longer believed possible. You can heal and rejuvenate far and away faster and better than you have ever been told, or lead to believe, this I know is true.

Never underestimate the power of the human hand when it is guided with love, intuition and imagination, especially in the heart of your home, your kitchen.

Now you can get to know my amazing partner Jay, and you will see why we encourage you to know what you are eating and to **Play With Your Food!**

We have also laid down some eye-opening science, ancient herbal wisdom and nutritional biochemistry about the food you are about to Sling.

So feed your brain and get a better understanding as to why the ice cream and pancakes you make for yourself, your family and friends from this book changes the game for the better.

"I am healthier now at 58 years old than I ever was at 38 years old. I have non-stop energy, sleep like a baby and I haven't any need for medications... not even an aspirin."

Growing up I didn't give much thought to what was "healthy" and what was "unhealthy." I grew up in the 1980s and 1990s, so I learned certain mass consciousness factoids, such as "fat is bad for you," although curiously enough, I knew from a very young age that my body loved fat and did very well with large amounts of it. Perplexing.

I was spoiled a bit, I always had high quality, home cooked meals. My dad is a chef, he has chefs and bakers on his side of the family tree, and my mom, though not a technically trained cook, can definitely hold her own in the kitchen, thanks to her Italian and Greek ancestry.

Much to my chagrin while growing up, my older sister Katherine and I were denied the delectable marshmallow-type breakfast cereals, and most of the other outrageously sugary and artificially flavored, processed western junk food that I was hypnotized into wanting to scarf down by the 40,000+ television commercials that influenced my young, susceptible mind each year while watching cartoons.

We mostly had the whole grain cereals, the most sugary flavor we ever got was honey nut. We had graham crackers in our lunch rather then candy, though we did have cookies, and on a special occasion, my mom's homemade cinnamon cake, which would make me the absolute envy of the elementary school lunch table.

After graduating from high school, I started studying yoga and because most of the serious yogis I read about were vegetarian, I went cold turkey vegetarian, which really was "junk food vegetarian." I still didn't have any awareness about food or about health, but I cut out a major dietary calorie source (which I still liked the flavor of very much) and so I naturally gravitated to the emerging market of meat-replacements, which back in the years 1999/2000 were all-soy, all-the-time. I still shudder when I think about the egregious estrogenic diet I ate during that period.

"Not only did I not know any of this, but up to this point, it didn't even occur to me that I should know any of this."

The junk food vegetarian years went on for about half a decade. In that time I strangely developed heart palpitations for the first time in my life while going to college in Boston and I got a referral to one of the top cardiologists in the entire city. What was he able to tell me? "It's probably genetic... I can start you on a medication if you want..." I was super confused. Aren't doctors supposed to know, like, everything? This guy didn't help one bit and he was the cardiologist for one of Boston's professional sports teams!

About a year or two after that, my dad was diagnosed with early stage prostate cancer, which he had taken out via operation. The human body was a mysterious thing, where anything seemed to be able to go wrong, and nobody seemed to know why.

The following year, as part of my yoga practice, I lived at an ashram up in the mountains of Quebec, Canada for several months.

Another practitioner at the ashram during that time was a psychologist from Germany, who was super enthusiastic about liver cleansing, bowel cleansing, and especially about the raw vegan diet. Within just a few conversations with him, it ignited an instant passion within me.

I couldn't believe that I had been alive for a quarter of a century, and I had NO IDEA how to take care of my body, not the first thing!

I didn't know ANYTHING about how the food I ate affected how I felt. Not only did I not know any of this, but up to this point, it didn't even occur to me that I should know any of this. All of a sudden I realized that the human body, while being miraculous, was not mysterious.

There are actually traditions from all around the world going back thousands of years, that know how to keep the body and the mind in a state of health and how to bring it back into a state of health if it is out of whack.

Things started making sense. I discovered that I had a subluxation (misalignment) in my neck, and it was likely the reason I had re-occurring ear infections as an infant. I realized that the ear infections I had as an infant, which resulted in many rounds of antibiotics in that critically early stage of life, was the reason I had what I now realized were multiple symptoms of candida overgrowth, which I had accepted as normal, because I had them quite literally my entire life.

As I continued on, I realized that the braces and the painful palatal expander that I had endured as a teenager were mechanically correcting classic signs of processed food and nutritional deficiency induced transgenerational bone formation degeneration. And in later years, I learned that just about all the conventional dental work I had received growing up, came with a very high bodily burden of toxicity.

All these things are normal in today's world, living on a toxified planet, being disconnected from nature, and consuming a diet of processed food-like-stuff. But just because it's normal, doesn't mean it's natural.

I eventually moved out to Los Angeles, California, and for seven out of the next ten years, I was immersed in the world of cutting-edge SuperFoods, Tonic Herbs and Tonic/Elixir Bars. I worked as an herbal consultant in Japan, I developed and managed the Tonic Bar for the LongevityNOW® Conferences and I spent much of that time "in the trenches," Slinging Jing with Truth Calkins at the famous Erewhon Market Tonic Bar in Hollywood.

So what is a Tonic Bar? Picture an alcohol bar, with hot drinks, smoothies and ice cream, but instead of alcohol and artificially flavored syrups, all the ingredients behind the bar are nutrient dense feel-good foods and herbs from around the world, the best of the best.

The Tonic Bar years were amazing. Creating custom elixirs with SuperFoods, Tonic Herbs and cutting edge supplements for dozens of clients every day, as they would whirl into Erewhon for an herbal pick-me-up, and then whirl back out into the matrix that is Hollywood, California, was an opportunity to develop and hone my craft unlike any other.

I had already been working with these amazing foods and herbs on my own for several years before this, but even making one elixir per day, it takes three years just to make 1,000. In this time period I surpassed a Malcolm Gladwellian 10,000 hours of mastery in crafting elixirs, creating, at last count, well over 50,000 custom Herbal Tonics, SuperFood Smoothies and SuperFood Ice Creams. I literally experienced 150 years worth of elixir creation time, compressed into less then a decade.

In addition to all my experience creating nutrient dense beverages, in those thousands of hours, I learned so much from my clients about how unique we are as individuals, truly there is no "one size fits all" when it comes to food and diet.

It was just after I returned from Tokyo, Japan five years ago, that Joy & I became the magic ingredients that created the recipe for the cookbook that you are now reading.

"A Tonic / Elixir is a hot drink, cold smoothie, or ice cream creation, made completely out of nutrient dense SuperFoods and enhanced with Tonic Herbs from around the globe."

So... what is Jing?

The very basic definition of "Jing" is that it is one's Essence. It's been written about for thousands of years throughout Taoist texts and used in Chinese Medicine. It's the foundational energetic force that comes together at the moment of conception, when sperm meets egg and a new life is formed. It is the palpable vibe you feel from someone who radiates health and strength.

For a modern metaphor, think of the comic book character Wolverine and his superpower called "Healing Factor." Essentially, Healing Factor is *unlimited* Jing! Wolverine has unlimited and immediate regeneration, an unlimited reservoir of healing energy. He doesn't age, so he is either immortal, or he has *extreme* longevity.

This is Jing. Jing is the energetic intelligence that instigates developmental changes in the body. It is the energy behind growth and regeneration. It is the energy of longevity. It is the creative and sexual drive. It is that inner strength in someone who has "good genes" and that deep vitality in someone who has a "strong constitution." Physically, Jing is related to the kidneys & adrenals. It's related to hormones, to the brain, to neurotransmitters, the spinal fluid and the reproductive fluid. It's the most refined Energy (Qi) in the body. It is what makes you, you.

Strong Jing combined with great nutrition creates physical beauty because the natural developmental changes and structure of the body are able to form to their highest potential, creating a mathematical symmetry and "beauty," that is everywhere in Nature, from a flower petal to a nautilus shell to the food that we eat.

"Nurture with Nature instead of Camouflaging with Chemicals. Now you can wield the Powerful Forces of Natures... deliciously."

Dipping the paintbrush of nature into the healing minerals from the earth and making those broad strokes from our dinner plate, begins to transform our body and restore aspects of our Jing. Utilizing these ancient secrets, that converge with brilliant natural science for beauty and optimum health, translates into vibrant longevity. This is the realm of the JingSlinger.

There is specific primal information waiting to be downloaded into your body from unadulterated organic foods, herbs and pure living water. This is the magic we will be sharing with you. The materials of the earth are the medium by which we have been created, and by which we live and breathe. We must engage these properties of the earth to restore and to thrive in our human form. "You are what you eat," has never been more true, or more important. Well-mineralized cells create healthy, robust tissue and the beauty on the inside is then reflected on the outside.

But it isn't just the physical texture of your skin that may improve. Your energy, libido, emotional states, and mental clarity all begin to transform when your physical vehicle receives proper nourishment and your Jing is fortified.

The symmetry and balance of a healthy body at any age is impressive to all of our senses. As JingSlingers, we know that clear eyes, shiny hair, and radiant skin are not elements exclusive to youth. In this day and age, we have at our immediate disposal, nature's palette of vivid, luscious organic foods, and the alchemical wisdom of SuperFoods and Tonic Herbs from around the world to allow us to be luminous.

When we talk about "Slinging the Jing" it's a playful way of saying that we are working hard, having fun and doing our dharma. It's about putting our life essence into our actions and doing what we know we are meant to be doing in this world, with passion and enthusiasm. We are happy and grateful for this opportunity to educate and illuminate the alchemical artist within you through our Clever Comfort Food recipes and simple secrets that even the busiest person can use, to help reclaim youthful radiance and energy. Time to Claim Your Chemistry, and get Jinged Up!

Jing

{Chinese} (n) One's essence; the foundational energetic force that comes together at the moment of conception; the energy of longevity and vitality which creates a person's constitution and instigates developmental changes in the human body; the sexual energy; the Source of Life; that which makes you, you.

JingSlinger

{JingLingo} (n) One who lives life with passion and integrity, allowing their true essence to shine through; a heart-centered alchemist of exceptional nutrition for body, mind and spirit. The epicenter of a JingMaster's wisdom is the synergistic mix and measure of cutting edge science, modalities and balancing natural remedies with SuperFoods from every corner of the world.

All of this is mindfully applied in concert with ancient global herbalism philosophies, bringing awareness that is fully in tune with the vibration to live in gratitude and harmony with our beautiful, abundant home... planet Earth.

Evolved Eating

"An ounce of prevention is worth a pound of cure." - Benjamin Franklin

As Tonic Herbalists and SuperFood Specialists we know that every day we have a choice about what we are going to eat and drink, and that this decision is one of compounding returns. When we are young, energetic and anabolic, we can get away with being more cavalier with our food choices, we have a lot more scooch room because our bodies are hormonal, rejuvenative, metabolic factories. We've got more Jing!

As we get older and wiser, it (should) become clear that we need to eat not only for today, but to eat also considering the effects for tomorrow and 10-20 years down the road. This is the tonic approach. Tonic Herbs are herbs that help to maintain and even re-establish homeostasis (balance) in a particular system of the body. They literally tonify, or strength, certain organs, tissues and/or systems of the body when taken over time and are perfectly safe to take for the long term.

This is the opposite end of the spectrum from taking a medicine, or even a medicinal herb. You should only need to take something that is "medicinal" for a short period of time when something in your body is already out of balance, until you are better.

Taking care of yourself each day is your most important responsibility. It is up to you, and no one else. Nourish yourself every day so that you can have steady energy, a strong immune system and neurotransmitters firing on all cylinders. An ounce of prevention each day, as Benjamin Franklin points out in the above quote, is far better then a bucketful of remedy when the body ends up in a big 'ol mess.

This cookbook is about showing you how to incorporate more nutrient dense food and beneficial herbs into your diet on a regular basis and showing you how to do it in a way so that you can still *enjoy* what you eat! What's the use of eating something that you think is "healthy" if every minute of it is a miserable experience?

Through the field of behavioral epigenetics, we are just beginning to learn that behaviors, stresses, and lack of nurturing in early childhood greatly affect our stress chemicals in adulthood.[1] So how do our behaviors, attitudes and associations about our food affect us?

If you are on the run and stressed out when you eat, you are triggering a fight-or-flight sympathetic nervous system stress response. Automatically your body channels energy away from your digestive track (digestion is part of a parasympathetic, rest-and-digest nervous system response), and to the peripheral of your body, the arms and legs. The idea of gathering around a dinner table with friends and family, giving gratitude for what you are about to eat, and eating in a relaxed state is the perfect environment for perfect digestion.

The stress of an on-the-go habit of wolfing down your food, or even the stress of hating the bland meal that you are only eating because you think you have to do it for your health, may very well have long term implications, not only affecting your genes, but affecting the genes in your lineage for generations to come. Chew on that!

We Encourage You to Play With Your Food!

We use terms like "SuperFood" and "Tonic Herb" throughout this cookbook, to denote certain foods and herbs that are revered for their nutrient density/chemical constituents and sometimes for their energetic qualities, though the two often go hand-in-hand.

In every part of the world, in every herbal tradition, certain foods and certain herbs are considered in the upper echelon above all others. But don't let that confuse or mystify you. Turmeric is still a spice, Cacao is still chocolate and Vanilla Bean is still delicious... it's all good!

Above all else, we want you to enjoy your food, have fun making it, feel great afterwards, and learn some of the science - if the science part interests you. Although this is a cookbook filled with recipes, we don't consider a recipe to be something chiseled in stone, we think of it more like a workable template.

We have been scientifically working with powerful ingredients for so long that, left to our own devices in the kitchen or behind a Tonic Bar, we rarely measure ingredients precisely. In fact, measuring out all of our ingredients was actually a challenge while writing this book! We are used to knowing the efficacy and also acting intuitively with food, which brings out more of the right-brained creativity of functional recipe design as a balance of alchemy and art. But just like any other art form, you first need to learn the basics, and certainly when making a dish for the first few times, it is important to have precise measurements...

So we got you covered there!

Everyone is Welcome at Our Table

Something unique about this cookbook is that we love to give you options! People follow different dietary guidelines for many different reasons. Maybe your ancestors ate a certain food, and your body is genetically wired to thrive on that food, whereas someone whose ancestors lived in a different climate or in a different part of the world are wired to thrive specifically with a different food. Maybe you have allergies to specific foods. Maybe you have had certain toxin exposure, and even the slightest trace amount of that toxin in your food supply gives you a reaction.

You may have moral or religious reasons for certain dietary guidelines. You could be in a certain stage of life and certain foods either do or don't work better for you now then when you were a teenager. Or perhaps you have a certain body type (e.g. Ayurvedic dosha) which influences which types of food, prepared in a certain way, work best for you. Maybe your *TAS2R38 taste receptor gene* indicates that you are a "super taster," or maybe your palate is not sensitive in the least.

We know... our serious science "geek-ery" is showing here, but hang with us. We want you to discover more about your individual primal blueprint and how to master it!

Whatever your reasons are for wanting to eat a certain way, we want to show you how to optimize and custom fit your choices to realize the results you really want.

We have included variations of the recipes in this book, so if you don't eat certain foods or food groups, we can still show you how to have the same type of final dish. When you have friends and family over, and there are a variety of diets at the table, everyone can have the same dish, with just a couple of different tweaks!

The common threads that we work with throughout the recipes in this book are that we show you how to make them Sugar-Free, Gluten-Free and Nutrient Dense. We specialize in using healthy low or non-glycemic sweeteners because over the years that is what has worked the best for us personally, and that is also what the majority of our clients need to feel and look great. We work with whole vegetables and fruits as much as possible, so some recipes do have the naturally containing sugars from the ingredients. If you prefer certain sweeteners that are not covered in this book, feel free to freestyle with what you love!

The Game Changed While We Weren't Looking

"For a modern disease to be related to an old fashioned food is one of the most ludicrous things I have ever heard in my life." - Dr. Thomas Latimer Cleave, Surgeon Captain (1906-1983)

There is a lot of confusion today about food, about what to eat and what not to eat. Every decade seems to make apologies for the food group that was demonized in the previous decade, only then to demonize something else. There's a principle at play that is important to understand...

It's not the food; it's what has been done to the food... and what has been done to the planet.

The planet has changed a lot in the last hundred years. Industry has changed our everyday dramatically in a lot of cool, techie ways, but it has also left an enormous toxic wake across the planet. In the soil, the air, the ocean, everywhere you look there are accumulated toxins that weren't around a century ago.

The free online video by the Environmental Working Group (EWG) called "10 Americans,"[1] explains about how umbilical cord blood, when tested for the first time ever, had an average of 212 industrial chemicals and pesticide breakdown products *that were banned over 30 years ago*. It had always been assumed that the placenta filtered out these toxins and the developing child in the womb wasn't exposed to them, but this unfortunately is not the case. Children today are actually born with a toxic load. But how does that happen?

Every year, about 21,000,000,000 pounds of known toxic chemicals are released into our environment by industries.[2] Of these, over 4,500,000,000 pounds are recognized carcinogens.[3] Aside from strategically planning on where we live, this is environmental exposure that we don't have much control over because it is ubiquitous.

The most recent figure from the Environmental Protection Agency (EPA) shows that in 2007 - 877,000,000 pounds of pesticides were used on crops in the United States alone.[4] An earlier statistic from 1999 shows that over 5,500,000,000 pounds of pesticides are used worldwide each year.[5]

Pesticide exposure IS something that we have A LOT of control over. Choosing organically grown food is an important first step.

Every year, the EWG publishes a list of their "Dirty Dozen" and "Clean Fifteen," which are the fruits and vegetables that are sprayed with the most, and the least amount of toxic chemicals. If it's on the "Dirty Dozen" list you absolutely want to buy it organic. If you are on a budget, or for availability purposes, you can get away with using some of the "Clean Fifteen" even if they are not organically grown.

Dirty Dozen

Apples Celery Cherry Tomatoes Cucumbers Grapes Nectarines Peaches Potatoes Snap Peas Spinach Strawberries Sweet Bell Peppers

* Hot Peppers. Kale/Collard Greens

Clean Fifteen

Asparagus Avocado Cabbage Cantaloupe Cauliflower Eggplant Grapefruit Kiwi Mangoes Onions Papayas Pineapples Sweet Corn Sweet Peas (frozen) Sweet Potatoes

The non-profit organization Pesticide Action Network has a website, www.whatsonmyfood.org which meticulously documents the pesticide residue found in fruits, vegetables, animal foods, and even in baby food. You can search by the type of food, or you can search by the type of pesticide. They even go so far as to show you the difference between the conventionally grown compared to the organically grown foods.

For example, on www.whatsonmyfood.org under "Baby Food - Applesauce," the first pesticide listed alphabetically is "Acetamiprid."

Acetamiprid:
Conventional Domestic Applesauce averages .4 micrograms, per 100 grams, with a high of 4.5 micrograms
Conventional Imported Applesauce averages 1.4 micrograms, per 100 grams, with a high of 5.0 micrograms
Organic Domestic Applesauce averages 0.0 micrograms, per 100 grams, with a 0.0 microgram high.[6]

We still don't know the many possible long-term effects that come with chronic pesticide exposure, but it has been shown that a number of pesticides act as xenoestrogens, artificially influencing the two main type of estrogen hormone receptors in the body.[7]

The effect of pesticide exposure on wildlife has been well documented and it's staggering. One of the most popular pesticides used today was shown by biologists at University of California, Berkeley to dramatically plummet fertility in male frogs and had such a massive endocrine disrupting effect, that 1 out of 10 male frogs actually transformed into female frogs![8, 9]

What was the dosage of the pesticide administered? 2.5 *parts per billion*. That's LESS then what is allowed by law in public drinking water.

Even better then buying organic, is buying LOCAL organic, at local farmers markets, or directly at the farm itself, if you live near one. By buying local and organic, you know that the food you are eating was taken out of the ground or off the tree within the last day or two. It hasn't been in cold storage for months, sprayed with synthetic plant hormones to retard the ripening process, or been irradiated while being imported into the country.

Buying locally also puts money directly into your community, and into the hands of smaller farmers with whom you can form a relationship every week at the market. Here are a few resources for tracking down local farmers markets in the United States:

http://www.localharvest.org/
https://www.farmstandapp.com/
http://www.farmerdirect2you.com/
http://www.ams.usda.gov/local-food-directories/farmersmarkets

Pesticides can disrupt the delicate balance of both the natural growth and the nutrition of plants in many ways. A number of plants have an "arbuscular mycorrhizal (AM) symbiosis" with certain types of fungi in the soil.[10] The fungi give the plant minerals in the soil through its roots and the plant in exchange gives the fungi carbon that it created by photosynthesis. Isn't that cool? This is an important part of the mineral uptake process for many plants and plants can suffer when this relationship is impaired by certain fungicides.[11]

Organically grown produce has also been shown to have higher levels of polyphenolic antioxidants then produce grown with pesticides. Why? Phenolics are actually produced as part of a plant's defense against bugs and pests, so a plant that has been sprayed with pesticides doesn't have to produce as many phenolics to defend itself.[12, 13] In selecting Chinese Herbs, master herbalist Ron Teeguarden has always said, "You want to pick the ginseng root that looks beat up, you want the one that has survived. It will have more of the beneficial compounds, and more Qi force."

Conventional fertilizing practices over the last century have also led to the depletion of many of the important minerals in the soil with the use of synthetic fertilizers and an emphasis on NPK (nitrogen-phosphorus-potassium) bases, as have selective breeding practices.

In a 51 year study (from 1940-1991), which was originally begun at Kings College University of London to test the chemical composition of foods over a decade earlier, it was shown that the foods tested in 1991, across the board, contained significantly less minerals then the same foods grown in 1940, with the only exception sometimes being the mineral phosphorus, which is one of the three featured in the NPK fertilizers.

"During the 51 year period Carrots lost 75% of their Magnesium, 48% of their Calcium, 46% of their Iron and 75% of their Copper, whilst our traditional 'spud' lost 30% of its Magnesium, 35% of its Calcium, 45% of its Iron and 47% of its Copper, and you would need to have eaten ten tomatoes in 1991 to have obtained the same copper intake as one tomato would have given you in 1940." [14]

The University of Texas at Austin's Department of Chemistry and Biochemistry published a similar study in 2004 in the *Journal of the American College of Nutrition*. They studied U.S. Department of Agriculture nutritional data from both 1950 and 1999 for 43 different vegetables and fruits, finding *"reliable declines" in the amount of protein, calcium, phosphorus, iron, riboflavin (vitamin B2) and vitamin C over the past half century. (They) chalk up this declining nutritional content to the preponderance of agricultural practices designed to improve traits (size, growth rate, pest resistance) other than nutrition."* [15]

Environmentally, NPK fertilizers and conventional farming practices have been a disaster. Excess nitrogen, phosphorus and wastewater run off pouring into the Gulf of Mexico has led to a massive "Dead Zone" of between 5,000-9,000 square miles in the ocean, creating "hypoxic" (very low oxygen) and "anoxic" (no oxygen) zones which cannot support most marine life. The US Geological Survey estimates that 101,000 metric tons of nitrates flowed down the Mississippi River, into the Northern Gulf of Mexico in the month of May 2014 alone. [16, 17]

We encourage you to support cleaner, healthier farming practices that create more nutrient dense crops. Buying organic is a good first step. Buying local organic is an even better second step. Best of all, grow your own food! If you have land, you can have a garden and if you don't have land, you can still have a garden!

Ron Finley, "The Guerrilla Gardener," has a great TED Talk on YouTube and a documentary called, "Can You Dig This Film," about how he transforms vacant lots in South Central Los Angeles into community gardens. He was instrumental in changing the law in Los Angeles to legalize the planting and maintaining of edible plants on public parkways. If he can do it in South Central LA, you can do it wherever you are.

When you grow your own food you have control and responsibility over the soil. You can re-mineralize the soil with something as simple as diluted ocean water or a sea salt solution. We use a worm composter. It can be stored either outdoors or indoors. Our worm composter is in the garage and it only takes up about one square foot. This means we always have organic fertilizer to support our patio garden. Our entire patio garden is in self-watering portable containers and yields about 45-50 pounds of organic veggies and fruit each season. These are grown from seeds we saved from our organic produce. Growing your own food is like growing your own money!

In case your are wondering, our patio is only 10' by 12' and the footprint for the garden containers are less than a quarter of that entire space. The sprouts, greens and herbs that we grow on our kitchen window sill are a bonus as we don't miss any of the live enzymes because they go right from the soil into the sandwich, salad or smoothie. Our personal garden favorite... our Goji bush. Yes, SuperFoods can be easy to grow on a patio and fresh Goji Berries are one of them!

Food for Thought

"In the last 75 years there was a gradual turning point in which our food went from primarily natural to primarily industrial.

So what does that mean?

The meals that our parents and grandparents consumed are not what we see on our plates today. The produce and meat may look the same to the naked eye, but the nutritional content is a mere shadow of its former self. So much of our conventionally produced food now carries components that confuse and can even highjack the necessary processes for a body to thrive."

"Most Americans eat the same 25-30 foods during their lifetime. Most of these foods are processed, carrying an unseen heavy toxic burden and are lacking the nutrient density we _think_ it has.

But! Add in SuperFoods, SuperHerbs, and switch to GMO-Free, Gluten-Free, Soy-Free, Processed Sugar-Free, Organic Whole Foods and clean Fats... and you have just Supercharged your Life."

You can eliminate the overload of unseen toxins that weasel their way into our everyday meals and stop these Silent Saboteurs by switching them out one by one.

The culprits, xenoestrogens in plastics, PTFE (Polytetrafluoroethylene) in older non stick and some new composite non stick cookware, aluminum foil & pans can leach *hormone high jacking* chemicals and heavy metals into our food. These synthetic elements migrate into our systems and can throw our mood, health and energy off track.

Old-School is the way to go, Grandma had it right. Cast iron skillets, stainless steel measuring cups, bowls and pans, along with glass baking dishes and wooden spoons are the better choice over plastics.

Now there are companies who specialize in 316 Titanium pans, ceramic dishes without lead issues and silicone molds that are safe to use in both hot or cold food preparation. The silicone is inert, meaning no leaching. We replaced things one at a time as our budget allowed and line bakeware with unbleached parchment.

Gear Up!

We do use foil BUT it never touches the food. Unbleached parchment paper is the secret here too.
We cover our oven-safe dishes with parchment paper then clamp it down with the foil if it needs to be sealed.

Did you ever notice how tin foil looks tarnished when you unwrap your baked potato or have you noticed actual tiny holes everywhere it touched your tomato sauce on your lasagna? That discolored foil etched and leached aluminum into your dinner.

We also do not use a microwave, not even to boil water or warm up food. We melt butter, coconut oil, palm shortening and chocolate in a double boiler or in a warm oven in an oven safe glass dish. Our microwave's only function is storage, it houses our clean dish towels, oven mitts and chef knives!

Food storage is always safer in glass. We save glass jars for storage and use Weck, Ball and Mason Jars that can be found at Target, Walmart or online.

Silicone Rolling Pin Rings will save you prep time and help you make a perfect crust or cookie every time!

Beyond the Plate...

Nice

We love the ease of using a digital heat gun instead of a messy candy thermometer :)

Know Your SuperFoods...

Every natural food that is part of the human diet can have a number of benefits, including macronutrients (fats, proteins & carbohydrates), vitamins, minerals, antioxidants and even more subtle energetic effects as well. Some foods though, pack a lot more power than others. Take a look at any culture and you will find there are always certain foods that are revered more than others based on knowledge from hundreds or even thousands of years of personal usage, that have been passed down through the generations. There will be story, lore and legend about these foods, stories about their origins, lore about the person who discovered them and legends about the profound effects they have. Reishi Mushroom, "the mushroom of immortality" may not actually grant you immortality, but it can help you to live a longer, healthier life by lowering NF-kb, a cellular trigger for inflammation that latches onto DNA and affects hundreds of genes. That's pretty cool!

Food is medicine and everything that you eat affects you in different ways. This is a guide of ancient wisdom and modern science about many of the foods we use throughout the recipe section of this cookbook. You will definitely recognize some of these foods and there may be ones that you are meeting for the first time. Fear not! If you are just starting out with SuperFoods and Tonic Herbs, you can simply take it one step at a time. Experiment with a new ingredient each week, or each month... or just dive right into the deep end with a whole bunch of them, it's up to you!

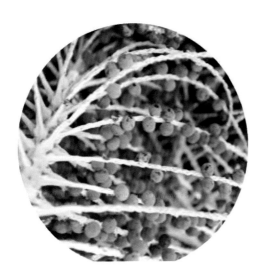

Acai

Acai (pronounced "ah-sigh-ee"), known as "the miracle fruit," is a palm tree berry from the Amazon. It is known for a plethora of amazing qualities, especially its anti-inflammatory effects. It Is the star in our "Triple Berry JingLato" or smoothie!

Its flavonoid velutin has been shown to influence the NF-kB pathway,[1] which is the cellular origin of the inflammation cascade and is linked with many immune system challenges. When Dr. Alexander Schauss studied Acai in the laboratory in 2006, he found that it had the highest antioxidant activity of any food ever recorded for certain free radical scavenging abilities.[2]

Apples

Apples are very rich in antioxidants, especially polyphenols in the apple skin, which is the way apples protect themselves from UV-B radiation.[1] They also contain chlorogenic acid, the fat burning compound found in green coffee beans.[2]

Apples are in season in the Fall, and are one of the great seasonal detoxification foods. Apples are rich in pectin, a soluble fiber, which is used for detoxifying the intestines, and have been shown to reduce low density lipoproteins (LDL).[3]

Aloe Vera

Aloe Vera is a desert dwelling succulent. Its use dates back 6,000 years, to early Egypt. Aloe is famous for its use in all types of topical applications on the skin, from helping with burns and wounds, to antimicrobial and antifungal activity. Its oral use has been shown to stimulate collagen and hyaluronic acid production by human dermal (skin) fibroblasts.[1] In Ayurveda, Aloe is known as "Kumari" which means "young girl/virgin," indicating its use as a rejuvenative for the female reproductive system, and as a libido enhancer.[2] Ayurveda uses Aloe Vera for issues of the liver, spleen and blood. It has a cooling, moistening nature, and is fantastic for adding into drinks designed to hydrate, such as our signature elixir "Living Waters Margarita" (page 142).

The bitter yellow compound called aloin, which is found in the inner skin, has laxative effects and needs to be diluted down in Aloe products. The gel itself also has gentle laxative qualities in higher doses, so start slowly when first introducing it into your diet.

Ashwagandha Root

Ashwagandha is one of the great "Rasayanas," in Ayurveda. Rasayanas are rejuvenative substances, the word translates as "that which enters the essence."[1] It has been used traditionally as a rejuvenative for the reproductive system, but especially for the nervous system and the brain. It is one of the best Vata balancing herbs, and is used to calm the nerves. It has also been used as a sleep regulator, taken over a period of weeks and months, to rebalance a person's nightly circadian rhythm.[2] This is probably at least in part because it has been shown to influence GABA signaling,[3] GABA being the major neurotransmitter that promotes calmness and relaxation.

Almonds

Almonds are a tree nut, native to the Middle East, that are high in many important trace minerals such as calcium, magnesium, manganese and phosphorus. It is also a great source of antioxidants, particularly the beauty enhancing Vitamin E family of antioxidants. In the Chinese and Ayurvedic herbal systems, Almonds are an important Jing/Ojas boosting food.

They have been used traditionally as a lung tonic and to help lubricate the intestinal tract. We sling Cultured Almond Cheese both sweet and savory in our "Holy Cannoli" (page 90) and our "Mac'N on the Qi'Z" (page 194).

Avocado

The Avocado fruit is native to Mexico and Central America, and there is evidence dating its use back nearly 10,000 years.[1] Its name comes from the Aztec word "ahuácatl," which means "testicle," owing to both its shape and its use as a libido booster in folk medicine. Avocados are rich in Vitamins B5 & B6, Vitamin C, Vitamin K, Folate, and the antioxidants Vitamin E, lutein and zeaxanthin.

It is also rich in monounsaturated fats, particularly oleic acid, an important omega 9 fatty acid. Oleic acid is the most abundant fatty acid in human breast milk, and is one of the fatty acid building blocks of myelin,[2] which is the insulation around our electrical nerves.

We spin this baby into "Bravocado" Superhero Chocolate Mousse (page 88), our "Guac Star" (page 183) and hundreds of other yummies!

Astragalus Root

Astragalus is the root of a short plant in the legume family. It has been used in Chinese Tonic Herbalism for over 2,000 years as an immune modulator, a lung and spleen tonic, and as a longevity enhancer. It improves many aspects of Qi, including the "Protective Qi," which is a part of the immune system, and "Upright Qi," which supports the body against the forces of gravity.

Astragalus has been shown to have modulating effects for Th1/Th2 immune imbalances.[1] It contains a number of tonic saponins, including Astragaloside IV, which is used in the patented supplement TA-65® and has been shown to slow down the shortening of, and even increase the length of telomeres.[2]

Telomeres are the end caps of our chromosomes, metaphorically likened to the plastic caps on shoes laces. They shorten a little bit every time a cell divides, thus acting like a countdown clock for cellular aging.

Brain Octane Oil

Bulletproof® Upgraded Brain Octane Oil™ is a special concentrate from coconut and/or palm oil of 8-carbon medium-chain triglycerides (MCTs). MCTs are fats that are quickly converted in the liver into ketone bodies, which are actually a preferred source of energy by the brain, over even glucose.

MCTs are used by people for nourishing the brain, cutting through brain fog, and enhancing the body's metabolism. This is one of the secret weapons in our "Love You Latte" (page 156) and "BLUcidity" Brain Shot (page 150).

Grass Fed Beef & Bison

Beef and Bison meat is the muscle meat of the animal. They are powerhouse superfoods containing important minerals such as iron, selenium and zinc as well as B Vitamins such as Vitamin B3 (niacin), Vitamin B6 and Vitamin B12. Humans have relied on this "red" meat as an essential food for Vitamin B12 and for building blood for at least 1.5 million years.[1] Muscle meat also contains creatine, an amino acid which can be converted into ATP (cellular energy) as well as the neuroprotective antioxidant carnosine.

Compared with beef that has been fed an unnatural inflammatory diet of grains, beef that has been fed a natural diet of grass has been show to contain higher levels of omega-3 fatty acids and conjugated linoleic acid, higher Vitamin A and Vitamin E precursors, and higher levels of the antioxidants glutathione and superoxide dismutase.[2]

Animal organs/glands have been consumed by humans throughout all recorded history and are actually the first thing eaten by wild animals when consuming fresh prey.

Organ and glandular extracts have been given in folk medicine to tonify and strengthen the like glands of the human body, dating back to ancient times in Egypt, India, and with Aristotle and Pliny in Greece.[3] In modern times, Dr. Royal Lee coined the term "protomorphogen" to describe specific compounds from a glandular extract product that are used as building blocks for those same organs in the human body.

Bison is much closer to a wild animal then beef. Bison meat is typically a little bit lower in fat content then beef and has a deeper, umami flavor. "Bison Charmed Chili" (page 202) is one of our most requested dishes.

Beet Root

Beetroots are an amazing food, used in folk medicine for nourishing the liver, gallbladder, spleen and kidneys. They are a natural source of healthy nitrates, which the body can convert into nitric oxide, the signaling molecule for opening up systemic blood flow. They are a source of B Vitamins, Vitamin C, and many important minerals, including the beauty boosting silicon, and testosterone boosting boron.[1]

Beets contain an amino acid called betaine, also known as trimethylglycine. Betaine is an important methyl donor, which recycles homocysteine, increases phase II liver detoxification,[2] is a powerful compound for eliminating excess estrogenic and xenoestrogenic compounds and even boosts serotonin levels.[3] Beets are also used for breaking down calcium deposits, building blood and moving the lymphatic fluid.[4] When you whip up our "Heart Beet Rawvioli,"(page 200) or our "Ribbon Salad" (page 181) you bring this beautiful root to crave-worthy status!

Broccoli

Broccoli was created through the selective breeding of wild cabbage, beginning as early as 2,500 years ago. It contains a compound called glucoraphanin, which is transformed into sulforaphane when chewed. Sulforaphane has been shown to be an epigenetic modulator, modulating DNA methylation, which in turn regulates gene expression.[1]

Like its close relative cauliflower, Broccoli creates indole-3-carbinol as a breakdown product, and supports overall liver and estrogen detoxification. Broccoli also contains chlorophyll and the important ocular antioxidants lutein and zeaxanthin.

Blueberries

Blueberries are known for their antioxidant content, their ability to improve night vision, and their ability to give apples a run for their money as the most popular pie filling. In a study involving veteran athletes, blueberries were also shown to not only reduce inflammatory markers, but also increase natural killer cells, which are a critical part of the body's immune system.[1]

When selecting Blueberries, we always choose the smaller sized, Wild Blueberries whenever available, oftentimes you can find them frozen. Wild Blueberries typically contain about double the amount of antioxidants as their organic, cultivated counterparts.[2]

Chaga Mushroom

Chaga is a hard, woody, dark black fungus (classified in the Hymenochaetaceae family) that grows on birch trees in northern climates around the world. Though is it sometimes thought to be a parasitic fungus, Chaga actually has a beneficial, symbiotic relationship with the birch tree.[1]

Chaga's dark color comes from its high melanin content. It has been used in folk medicine for centuries as both an immune system enhancer, and for many types of skin issues. It has been shown to be highly effective against tough conditions like psoriasis, when taken over a 2-3 month period.[2] Its effect on the immune system comes from a variety of very powerful compounds, such as 1,3 beta glucans and betulinic acid.[3]

Cacao Bean

Theobroma Cacao, whose name means "Food of the Gods," is technically the seed of the Cacao Fruit. It is grown in many tropical climates around the world, but is native to South America, where its use has been traced back over 3000 years.[1] It is loaded with a staggering array of nutrients and complex compounds. It contains important minerals such as calcium, chromium, iron, magnesium, and zinc, as well as many different types of antioxidants.

It contains numerous neurotransmitters such as PEA (see "Brain On") and anandamide, which is known as the "bliss chemical," and is a cannabinoid neurotransmitter that activates dopamine receptors. Cacao also contains the amino acid tryptophan, which is a precursor to serotonin. In addition, Cacao contains monoamine oxidase inhibitors, which slow down the recycling of neurotransmitters, allowing them to have a longer effect in the body.

Cacao does contain the stimulants theobromine, caffeine and theophylline, containing much less of the latter two.[2] These compounds make Cacao a great vasodilator, and fantastic for combining with additional SuperFoods and Tonic Herbs for better absorption. People who are sensitive to stimulates may need to take it slow with Cacao. Most people are good with it in moderate amounts, but it can be too stimulating for people with extremely sensitive nervous systems.

Candy Cap Mushroom

Candy Caps are a delicious little mushroom that are famous for tasting uncannily like maple syrup due to a compound called sotolon. Sotolon, though created naturally by the Candy Cap, is actually the chemical used by makers of fake maple syrups to impart that distinct mapley flavor.[1] Its flavor may be where conventional wisdom ends for the Candy Cap, but those who have enjoyed eating it, or consumed its blue pigmented extracts, know that the scientific understanding of this tasty little fellow has only just begun. Candy Caps can have astounding mood uplifting, brain boosting, heart opening and laugher/goofiness enhancing effects, so much so that people who are very sensitive to the effects of food and energy should start with small amounts. Try them in our Panacea Panna Cotta (page 96), silliness may ensue!

Cassava Root

Cassava Root (also known as "yuca") was a staple food in pre-Columbian South America and is today a staple food for about 500 million people around the world. It is a hardy plant, which can grow in very dry, barren soil. When the starch of Cassava Root is extracted, it is known as Tapioca Starch. It is starchy like a white potato but is much better tolerated by people with nightshade sensitivities. When processed correctly, Cassava makes an amazing, gluten-free baking flour. It is light, fine and its texture mimics traditional flour.

Otto's Cassava Flour is our favorite. It can usually be used seamlessly cup for cup in recipes that call for conventional flour. It is amazing in our Pâte À Choux when making our "Epic Éclairs" (page 130) that are a Paleo, Grain-Free triumph! Beignets and other fine pastries also become possible with Cassava flour, especially when mixed with other Grain-Free or Gluten-Free flours.

Cashews

Cashews are rich in a number of important minerals such as copper, iron, manganese, magnesium and zinc, but their real claim to fame, other then their amazing taste, is their high tryptophan content. "Several handfuls of cashews provide 1,000-2,000 milligrams of tryptophan, which will work as well as prescription antidepressants," says Dr. Andrew Saul, a therapeutic nutritionist and editor-in-chief of the Orthomolecular Medicine News Service. The body turns tryptophan into serotonin, a major neurotransmitter of sexual desire, good mood, and healthy sleep.[1]

We like to soak cashews, discard the soak water and blend them into anything as a creamy component.

Cauliflower

Cauliflower is a cruciferous vegetable, consumed by humans for at least 2500 years and native to the eastern Mediterranean. Like its close relative broccoli, Cauliflower was created by selectively breeding wild cabbage over a long period of time. Cauliflower contains sulfurous glucosinolate compounds, which break down into important immune system supporting and detoxification products like sulforaphane, raphanin and indole-3-carbinol.[1]

Cauliflower is rich in flavonoids and many other antioxidants like Vitamin C and a variety of B Vitamins, including choline, the building block for the neurotransmitter acetylcholine, as well as a building block for the fat that makes up our cell membranes, phosphatidylcholine. It is the superstar ingredient in our "GlowTatoes" (page186).

Chanca Piedra

Chanca Piedra is a green leafy Amazonian herb whose name literally means "Stone Breaker."

It has a number of traditional uses, including use against many types of infection.[1] However, Chanca Piedra is most famous for what it name implies, it has been shown effective for preventing calcium oxide crystal formations in the body[2,3] and has been used in traditional herbalism for assisting in the breakdown of crystallizations and stone-like buildups in the body. It is tonic and protective of both the liver and the kidneys. We love to use it as a tea.

We have had clients who have rendered conventional kidney stone procedures unnecessary by drinking Chanca Piedra tea as part of their daily water intake.

Carrot Root

Carrots have been consumed for at least 5,000 years. They have been used traditionally to strengthen the lungs, spleen and pancreas[1] and have been shown to have liver protective qualities.[2]

Carrots are most famous for their high content of beta-carotene, a Vitamin A (retinol) precursor. The conversion of beta-carotene to retinol is dependent upon a number of factors, including a person's genetics, as well as having enough high quality fat in the diet, as Vitamin A is a fat-soluble nutrient. Carrots contain numerous additional antioxidants, especially in the darker pigmented varieties, including lutein, lycopene and anthocyanins.

Chia Seeds

Chia Seeds are an heirloom Superfood from Central and South America, which have been eaten for over 5,000 years. They have been used as an endurance food and contain a great balance of fats, proteins and carbohydrates. They are a staple food for the Tarahumara Indians of northwestern Mexico, the famed tribe of elite distance runners in the NY Times Bestselling book "Born to Run."

Due to their high soluble fiber content, they will expand and gelatinize in water, creating filling drinks that keep your hunger satiated for hours. They are extremely hydrophilic, absorbing nearly 10x their weight in water, so always consume plenty of liquids with them. Because of their hardness and their tendency to get stuck in between teeth, we recommend making a Chia gel with them first, rather then consuming them raw. We use chia gel in vegan baked goods as an egg replacement (page 136) and to make our Chia Pudding (page 94).

Coconut Meat & Coconut Oil

Coconut Meat is a good source of Vitamin C and contains a number of important minerals such as iron, magnesium, manganese, and selenium. Coconut Water is an excellent, hydrating source of electrolytes. It naturally contains about 12 grams of sugar per cup, so it is not appropriate for people on a low sugar or antifungal diet, but you can ferment Coconut Water (page 158) with a probiotic starter culture and produce Coconut Water Kefir. You can also buy it in the refrigerated probiotic section of health food stores. Coconut Water Kefir is rich in live probiotics who have multiplied and eaten many of the sugars in the Coconut Water, leaving a sour, and bubbly final result. Coconut Water Kefir is the important base for our "Living Waters Margarita" (page 142).

In addition to the brain and metabolism boosting effects from the MCTs found in Coconut Oil (see "Brain Octane Oil," page 36), the main fatty acid found in Coconut, lauric acid, is tremendously beneficial for the immune system. Lauric acid gets converted in the body into monolaurin, a compound that has been shown since the 1960s to be a powerful antimicrobial.[1] Coconut Oil has also been shown to be an effective antifungal agent against a variety of candida species.[2]

Colostrum

The Colostrum of other animals has been utilized in Ayurveda and consumed for thousands of years all around the world. It is quite literally the original SuperFood. It is the "super milk" that mammals produce in the first 24-48 hours after giving birth to nurse a new life. Colostrum is rich in powerful immune system compounds such as lactoferrin, interferon and all five classes of immunoglobulins.[1]

Colostrum is perhaps the single most anabolic, rejuvenative food found in nature. It contains insulin-like growth factors (IgF-1 and IgF-2), an epithelial growth factor (EgF), transforming growth factors (TgF-A and TgF-B), and a platelet-derived growth factor (PDGF).[2] Like with milk, colostrum is most powerful in its raw, live state, though it is most commonly found and used in a powderized state. We Sling the powder into our "BuckShot" SuperFood Icing (page 89).

Coffee Beans

Did you know that Coffee is the number one source of antioxidants in the American diet? The caffeine in Coffee has been shown to have numerous positive effects on the body, including for mental performance, brain health, and mood,[1] as well as being extremely protective against neurodegenerative diseases later in life.[2]

People with caffeine sensitivities need to gauge how much Coffee they can consume. Some people can drink Coffee and take a nap, while other people who have sensitive nervous systems can't drink it at all. Most people are in between these two extremes.

Another issue with Coffee, as with Cacao, is trace amounts of mycotoxicity from mold.[3, 4, 5] Some people may not notice small amounts of mycotoxicity in the food they consume, but other people, depending on their previous exposure to mold, the effectiveness of their detox pathways and genetic mutations, may react severely to even trace amounts. Our favorite mindfully mold-less coffee is Bulletproof®.

Celery

Celery has been used traditionally as a tonic for the liver, the kidneys, the blood and the bones. It has a naturally high sodium and silicon content, as well as nutrients like Vitamin K1. It contains many antioxidants and anti-inflammatory compounds, including apiuman, a type of pectin. Celery contains a unique compound called butylphthalide, which has been shown to lower blood pressure and cholesterol levels.[1] Add it to your savory dishes and soups for fat-burning, your body uses a bit more energy to break down this unsung hero and it provides awesome fiber for good digestion.

Collagen

Collagen is the most abundant protein in the human body, making up about 30-40% of the total protein content.[1] It is a major component of connective tissue, as well as tendons, cartilage, ligaments, bones and skin, the latter of which has earned it a reputation as a top beauty food. It is a secret of our red carpet clients, helping to keep skin plump and strong, even into advanced age. We prefer bovine collagen over fish or avian. It is vitally important that it is derived from clean grass-fed animals.

The most abundant amino acid in Collagen is glycine. Glycine is a fantastic anabolic amino acid, and has been shown to increase both human growth hormone and hemoglobin production.[2]

Dragon Fruit

Dragon Fruit, or Pitaya, is a unique cactus fruit, native to Central and South America. The outside of the fruit can be various shades of pink, yellow or green, with large scales, the type you would expect to find on a dragon.

The flesh inside will be either white or a bright magenta. The magenta variety contains a number of beneficial compounds called betacyanins, which are the same compounds that give beetroots their dark red color. One of the betacyanins, betanin, has been shown to be a potent immune system enhancer against certain types of mutagenic cells.[1]

Both types of Dragon Fruit contain oligosaccharides, specific sugars that feed the beneficial bacteria in your digestive tract. The oligosaccharides in Dragon Fruit have been shown to feed both lactobacilli and bifidobacteria probiotics.[2] Pitaya makes for an easy antioxidant breakfast when Slung into our Pitaya Bowl (page 172).

Free Range Organic Chicken

The domestication of wild chickens began about 5,000 years ago.[1] Chicken meat, in addition to being protein dense, contains the omega-3 fatty acids EPA and DHA. It is rich in B Vitamins, particularly the circulatory enhancing Vitamin B3 (niacin) and blood building Vitamin B6. It is a great source of the mineral selenium, which is crucial for creating glutathione, your body's most powerful intracellular antioxidant.

43

Cricket Flour

Crickets are a complete protein, containing all nine essential amino acids. They contain double the amount of protein by weight as beef, and are rich in important minerals such as magnesium and iron. Even more importantly, crickets (and all edible insects) are whole foods because the entire insect is consumed, not just the muscle meat, so by consuming Cricket Flour, we also consume all the beneficial organs and glands, adding an important type of nutrition back into our diet. We Sling Cricket Flour into our "Guru Goji Brilliant Brownies," (page 116) but there's no crunchy antenna bits in there!

Entomophagy is the eating of insects, something that is commonplace for about 80% of the world's population,[1] but only now is beginning to break into the diet of the western world, especially since the Food and Agriculture Organization of the United Nations released their report in 2013 entitled, "Edible Insects: Future Prospects for Food and Feed Security." About 1,900 different species of insects are consumed by humans around the globe.[2] "Crickets are the gateway bug." Megan Miller, founder, Bitty Foods.

Gynostemma

Gynostemma (aka Jiaogulan) is a green leafy plant in the same family as the cucumber. It is grown in certain parts of Asia, including China and Japan where it has been studied extensively. It is a premiere longevity tonic herb in the Chinese/Taoist Tonic Herbal system and is a first class adaptogen. You can drink Gynostemma Tea in the morning, and it can help give you an energy boost, while you can drink it in the evening and it can help you wind down for bed. It has been shown to improve many factors related to physical stress, exercise and fatigue.[1] It has also been shown to have neuroprotective effects,[2] hypoglycemic effects, and to increase important antioxidant systems like SOD and Glutathione.[3] It's natural chemical compounds, called gypenosides, are saponins, very similar (and some actually identical) to those found in Ginseng, though Gynostemma has more then double the variety of saponins when compared to Ginseng. We use Gynostemma Tea ice cubes as a brilliant JingLato base. Sling That!

Ghee

Ghee is a purified, clarified butter, made from heating butter and removing the proteins, lactose and water. It is the ultimate SuperFood in Ayurvedic medicine and Ayurvedic cooking, and is a phenomenal builder of Jing/Ojas. Ghee is rich in fat-soluble nutrients, including Vitamins A, D, E and K2. It is one of the most concentrated forms of butyric acid, an important short chain fatty acid which is created by the bacteria in the colon and is the preferred energy source for the epithelial cells that line the colon.[1] Ghee is also one of the highest natural sources of conjugated linoleic acid, an immune system and metabolizing boosting fatty acid.

Ghee is used both internally and externally and is used especially for detoxification. It has been used in Ayurvedic cleanses to lubricate and soften hardened tissues, as well as stimulate bile production, mitigate fat-soluble toxins and boost a fat burning metabolism.[2] Ghee has a high smoke point, over 450 degrees Fahrenheit, making it an ideal oil for cooking. Our numero uno brand of Ghee for many years has been Ancient Organics. The buttery, toffee flavor is second to none.

Goji Berry

Goji Berry is a small red berry, native to China. It is a premiere Yin Jing and blood replenisher and is packed with carotenoids. In tonic herbalism, it is used as a longevity herb, for regulating the immune system, for improving libido and fertility, as well as improving one's mood.

In studies Goji Berry has been shown to increase sperm quantity and mobility in rats,[1] increase natural killer cells in humans,[2] enhance T-lymphocyte, B-lymphocyte and macrophage functions[3] and reduce inflammation via the NF-kB pathway.[4]
The fresh Goji Berries you see in Jay's hand on the left were grown right on our patio... free SuperFoods! Our "Goji Balsamic Dressing" (page 175) deliciously Jings-Up any salad or dish.

Eggs

When we reference eggs throughout this book, we will be talking about pasture-raised chicken eggs, though we love duck eggs too! Depending on where in the world you live, cultures consume eggs of all types, from fish eggs, to ant eggs, to ostrich eggs. Eggs are one of the most nutritious foods on the planet. Both the white and the yolk have different advantages, but most of the good stuff is in the yolk. Eggs contain the eye-centric antioxidants lutein and zeaxanthin, they contain DHA, lactoferrin, growth factors, fat soluble vitamins like Vitamin D, Vitamin A (the active, retinol form), B Vitamins, such as choline, Vitamin B12, folate, and minerals such as iron, phosphorus and selenium. They also contain Lecithin (see the section on Lecithin).

Eggs are a good source of healthy dietary cholesterol. The majority of cholesterol in our bodies, about 80%, is produced by our liver.[1] High cholesterol is often a sign of inflammation in the body, not from having healthy cholesterol in your diet.

Jay Foster, a nutritional biochemist we work with in Miami, Florida, once had a new client, a 54 year old man, who had a whopping triglyceride count of 3,395 and a total cholesterol of 625 when tested! Those levels were confirmed by a second round of tests by the man's conventional doctor. Jay had the man cut out most of his carbohydrates and dairy for 30 days and add in some strategic supplements. The man loved eggs and Jay had told him, "Eat as many eggs as you want, just don't eat carbs with them," so the man ate three eggs at every meal, three times per day during the 30 days. At the end of 30 days, his triglycerides dropped all the way down to 149 and his total cholesterol dropped to 170... On 9 eggs per day!

He Shou Wu Root

He Shou Wu (aka Polygonum Multiflorum; though sometimes mislabeled as "Fo-Ti") is one of the greatest kidney Yin/adrenal replenishing, liver protective and longevity herbs used in Tonic Chinese Herbalism. Its name translates to mean "Mr. Black Hair," owing to its fame for being able to bring back a person's original hair color after turning gray. Its hair color enhancing qualities are likely due to its ability to increase the body's very important super oxide dismutase (SOD) antioxidant system.[1] He Shou Wu must be "prepared" meaning that it is cooked with black beans. This transforms the raw root, which would otherwise be a laxative, into one of the greatest tonic herbs in the world. We use the already prepared powdered extract. Joy loves it, and has experienced less gray hair by adding it to her morning tea, coffee and smoothies.

Garlic

Garlic is an ancient SuperFood. It has a long history of human use from all around the world in ancient China, Egypt, Greece and India.[1] It has been used traditionally against virtually every type of opportunistic organism infection, due in large part to its sulfurous compound call allicin. It is classified in Ayurveda as a "rasayana," or rejuvenative, and is used to enhance libido and sperm count.[2] Its heating qualities are useful as an expectorant, but can also imbalance people who have a naturally hot constitution.

Garlic is classified in Ayurveda as being "tamasic," meaning it can dull the mind. For this reason (in addition to its libido boosting ability), it, along with onions have been discouraged in many meditation traditions throughout history. James Hardt, PhD actually says in his book "The Art of Smart Thinking," that consuming garlic and onions make it more difficult for a person to achieve relaxed Alpha brain waves.[3]

Black Garlic is garlic that has been aged for 30 days in a specific climate of heat and humidity, and then aged for another 30-45 days outside of that climate. The garlic completely transforms into a dark black, soft, rich, sweet and earthy tasting food. The allicin content is much lower but the content of another compound, S-Allylcysteine is more then 10 times higher then in raw garlic. S-Allylcysteine has been shown to have neuroprotective effects against various forms of damage, including amyloid-beta peptides.[4, 5]

Ginger Root

Ginger is a well-known herb around the world, and has been used especially in Indian and Asian cuisine for over 4,000 years. It has been used traditionally in a wide range of uses for digestion, including upset stomachs, diarrhea, and nausea[1]. Some of Ginger's compounds such as 6-gingerol and 6-Shogaol have been shown to be highly effective against certain types of mutated cells and even against types of mutated stem cells[2,3,4].

Jungle Peanuts

Jungle Peanuts are a clean, heirloom variety of the legume from South America. Peanut allergies have been dramatically on the rise in recent years.[1] Modern peanuts are very susceptible to inflammatory aflatoxin exposure from mold. We have found that some people who have reactions to conventional peanuts, are able to consume heirloom jungle peanuts without incident (but always check with your doctor first!).

Peanuts are one of the highest natural sources of Biotin (Vitamin B7, aka Vitamin H), which is known as the "hair vitamin." They are also rich in healthy monounsaturated fats, and even contain small amounts of resveratrol.

Lion's Mane Mushroom

Lion's Mane, also known as the Pom Pom Mushroom, is a tree mushroom with some very unique neuro enhancing properties, it contains two compounds, hericenones and erinacines, which stimulate nerve growth factor in the body.

The 1986 Nobel Prize was awarded for the research on nerve growth factor, a protein the body produces for growth, maintenance and regeneration of certain neurons.[1] Lion's Mane has also been shown to reduce beta amyloid plaque in the brain, and to reverse the symptoms of the damage caused by amyloid plaque.[2]

In addition to its neurological properties, Lion's Mane has been shown to have immune system, cardiovascular, and a wide range of protective and beneficial effects throughout the body.[3]

Kelp

Kelp, or Kombu, is a seaweed that is a nutritional powerhouse and is the highest natural source of the mineral iodine. Iodine is the mineral your thyroid your uses, along with the amino acid tyrosine, to create thyroid hormones.

Your two major thyroid hormones are Triiodothyronine, or T3, which has three atoms of iodine in its structure, and Thyroxine, or T4, which has four atoms of iodine in its structure. Kelp is a tremendous Yin food, it's fantastic for kidney/adrenal replenishment. High doses of Kelp can leave you in a very relaxed, and sleepy state. It is featured in our nighttime "Miso Yin" Soup (page 152).

Lecithin

Lecithin is a group of phospholipids, composed of units of choline, phosphoric acid, fatty acids, and glycerol.[1] Phospholipids, such as phosphatidylcholine and phosphatidylserine are critical fats that make up our cellular membranes. The word "Lecithin" comes from the Greek word meaning "egg yolk," which is where it was first isolated. The choline in Lecithin is a building block for acetylcholine, the brain's major neurotransmitter for memory.

Culinarily, Lecithin is used to emulsify (break down) fat/oil, so it will blend with water-based ingredients. Most Lecithin extracts on the market are derived from soy, but we prefer to use a Sunflower Lecithin Powder. If you are going to buy a soy derived Lecithin, make sure it is non-GMO and get the soy powder rather then the soy granules, because they will be less estrogenic.

Maca Root

Maca is a South American root vegetable that grows at high altitudes in the Andes Mountains, famous for its energy, aphrodisiac and fertility enhancing properties. When the Spanish first came to South America and their livestock had low reproduction rates, they fed them Maca upon the suggestion of the local Native Americans, and recorded in their travel logs the profound results.[1] Maca has been shown in studies to help reverse SSRI induced sexual dysfunction[2] and also to enhance sperm count in men.[3]

Traditionally Maca is consumed by being used as a baking flour, or the fresh roots will be roasted whole. When buying and using it as a smoothie ingredient, it's best to get a brand that is "pre-cooked" or "gelatinized." These processes break down the dense fiber in the Maca, make the minerals and nutrients more bioavailable and make Maca easier to digest. Although it possesses adaptogenic qualities, Maca is quite warming, so people with a hot constitution do need to be mindful of that.

Lucuma Fruit

Lucuma Fruit (Pouteria Lucuma), also known as Egg Fruit, is native to areas of South America, including Peru, Ecuador and Chile. It has been consumed for thousands of years has been a staple food for cultures such as the Inca. It contains many trace vitamins, minerals, and antioxidants, including beta-carotene, Vitamin B3, Vitamin B6, Vitamin C and iron.

Culinarily, Lucuma is very versatile. It has a creamy-mapley-caramelly flavor. We use it in a number of recipes to impart a unique flavor and sweetness to hit your palate just right. It is some of the magic in our "PB by Jay" JingLato (page 102) and our "SuperFood Salted Caramel Sauce" (page 76).

Mucuna Pruriens

Mucuna, known as Kapikacchu in Ayurveda, and also known as Velvet Bean in North America, is a top reproductive and nervous system rejuvenative and Jing/Ojas builder. It contains a number of amino acids and neurotransmitters for the brain, such as L-Dopa, serotonin, N,N-DMT, and bufotenine.[1]

Owing to its L-Dopa concentration, a precursor for the neurotransmitter dopamine, it has been used in Ayurveda for many different types of nervous system conditions. Traditionally it has been used as both a male and female reproductive tonic, and has been shown to boost dopamine, testosterone, luteinizing hormone, as well as sperm count and sperm motility in infertile men.[2]

This lovely bean-flavored herb gets slung into chocolate, salad dressings and other savoury recipes like our wildly popular "Charmed Chili" (page 202).

Pearl

Pearl Powder has been one of the beauty secrets of Tonic Chinese Herbalism for the last 2,000 years and remains one of the top beauty secrets in Hollywood today. Pearl contains a number of beautifying trace minerals and amino acids, as well as mucopolysaccharides (also known as glycosaminoglycans, or GAGs), which are one of the components that make up the dermis, along with collagen and elastin.[1] Pearl Powder also increases the ever-important antioxidant superoxide dismutase.[2]

Pearl is one of the greatest calming and grounding substances in tonic herbalism. It is a premier Shen stabilizer, helping to center a person's mood and help them to cope with stress. It has virtually no taste and can be incorporated seamlessly into nearly any recipe. It is fantastic in nighttime recipes, such as our "Sleeping BeauTea" (page 157).

Psyllium Husk

Psyllium Husk is part of the seed from the Plantago Ovata plant, native to India and Pakistan. It is a very rich source of soluble fiber and is used as a supplement to help with constipation and bowel cleansing issues. It absorbs large amounts of water and acts as a bulking agent, as well as a stool softener. It is also used to lower blood sugar and cholesterol levels[1].

Culinarily, we sometimes use it in place of eggs in vegan recipes and as a binder in Gluten-Free baking. It is an effective appetite suppressant and also helps to detoxify the body.

Pomegranate Fruit

Pomegranates are a revered ancient food, they are mentioned in many of the oldest written texts, including Babylonian texts, the Bible, the Quran, Egyptian papyrus, Tang Dynasty characters, Greek Mythology and ancient Armenian texts.[1]

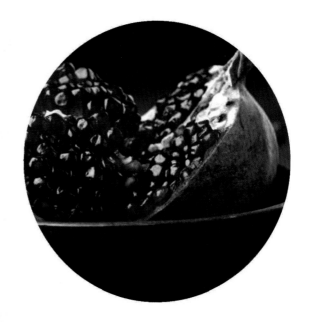

They contain powerful antioxidants called punicalagins, as well as punicic acid, a unique omega-5 fatty acid that has been shown to have remarkable effects on both estrogen sensitive and estrogen insensitive mutagenic cells.[2] Pomegranate juice has been shown to have anti-inflammatory effects for type 2 diabetics.[3]

Pomegranate juice is the base for our antioxidant powerhouse "Jing Jam," (page 80) one of our most versatile Superfood yummies! Extra bonus... it is a one-bowl, one-spoon recipe!

Probiotics

Our bodies have a symbiotic relationship with thousands of different types of beneficial bacteria, so much so that the number of bacteria cells in our body actually outnumber human cells by a factor of 10-to-1. Probiotics are crucial for maintaining the health of our skin, but especially for the health of our digestive and immune systems. You will find the power of probiotics in our drinks, our desserts, sides and entrees.

Beneficial bacteria produce many important nutrient byproducts such as butyrate, a short-chain saturated fatty acid which can help decrease intestinal permeability and has been shown to increase energy expenditure and improve insulin sensitivity.[1] Probiotics are a crucial part of our enteric nervous system and can even enhance neurotransmitters. The bacteria lactobacillus rhamnosus has been shown to regulate GABA receptor expression.[2]

You will find probiotic recipes throughout this book. Sweet recipes like our Holy Cannoli (page 90), drinks such as our Living Waters Margarita (page 142) and savory delights like our Immortal Gut (page 182).

Pumpkin Seed/Pumpkin Seed Oil

Pumpkin Seeds, native to South America, have a long history of human usage for the past 10,000 years, as squashes are one of the "Three Sisters," the three staple crops of the Native Americans. Pumpkin Seeds have long been used in herbology as an anthelmintic both for humans and animals.[1] They are rich in a number of vitamins, antioxidants and in the anabolic, testosterone boosting minerals magnesium and zinc.

Pumpkin Seeds, and particularly Pumpkin Seed Oil, have been shown to be supportive of good prostate health.[2] Pumpkin Seed Oil is rich in chlorophyll, which gives it its deep dark green color. Our favorite Pumpkin Seeds and Pumpkin Seed Oil is the Styrian variety from Austria. It's our secret ingredient for imparting a rich, peanut buttery flavor into recipes without using peanuts, like in our "PB By Jay" (page 102).

Quinoa

Quinoa (pronounced "Keen-wah"), whose name means "mother," is a highly adaptive gluten-free "pseudocereal," which is able to thrive in very extreme weather conditions.[1] It was a sacred, staple food of the Inca in South America and has been consumed for over 5,000 years.

Quinoa contains many important minerals such as iron, magnesium and zinc. It is a complete protein, containing all nine essential amino acids and contains a high amount of antioxidants such as the flavonoids quercetin and kaempferol. It has been shown to lower inflammation in adipose (fat) tissue and in the intestinal tract.[2] It is the nutritional springboard for our Quiona Risotto (page 206) and it is puffed quinoa that gives our "SlingShots" (page 126) that special *uber* protein packed crunch.

Reishi Mushroom

Known as "the king of herbs," Reishi Mushroom is a Tonic Chinese Herb, but it grows all over the world, including throughout North America. Reishi is a true adaptogen, it helps the body to handle all forms of stress (physical, chemical, emotional and energetic) and actually helps to regulate systems of the body, including the immune system, while protecting against DNA damage.[1]

It physically nourishes the organ systems, especially the liver and the heart, but it also deeply nourishes on a mental and emotional level. It is a supreme Shen stabilizing herb. It helps to balance emotions in an immediate way and is known for its deep spiritual qualities, imparting wisdom to those who take it over long periods of time. These qualities have earned it the name, "the herb of good fortune," as people who consume Reishi on a regular basis are said to literally have more luck flow their way.

Rose

Rose flower petals have been used for their fragrance in baths going back to ancient Rome. The essential oil is used for its antibacterial and anti-inflammatory effects. Rose is one of the great Shen stabilizing herbs, it is used for calming, centering, and for (energetically) opening the heart. It is no wonder that we have such a connection with giving a bouquet of Roses to express our love.

Rose Hips, the fruit of the plant, is one of the highest Vitamin C containing foods and can be used in blended drinks or in tea. Our favorite culinary form of Rose to use in the kitchen is a high quality organic Bulgarian Rose Water. Organic Rose petals are wonderful to eat and to use as an edible decoration.

Sesame Seeds

Native to both India and Africa, human consumption of Sesame Seeds dates back at least 5,000 years. Both White and Black Sesame Seeds are high in many important minerals including calcium and copper.

Black Sesame Seeds have been used in Chinese Medicine for nourishing the liver and the kidneys. It is a Jing building and youthening food, helping to strengthen the hair and return it to its original color. Both kinds of seeds are used to lubricate the bowels, while White Sesame Seed is also used to moisten the skin.[1] They contain a number of antioxidants and have been shown to raise plasma Vitamin E levels.[2] The hulls of sesame seeds contain a high amount of oxalates, so people who have impaired intestinal tracts should get the hulled variety.

Rice

Rice fuels over 50% of the world's population. It is a symbol of wealth, health and fertility, which is why it is traditionally thrown at weddings.[1] Our two favorite types of rice are Purple/Black "Forbidden" Rice and White Basmati Rice.

Purple/Black "Forbidden" Rice was once reserved only for Chinese royalty. Its dark color is due to its anthocyanin content, well-studied pigments which have been shown to have numerous benefits, including anti-inflammatory and immune modulating effects.[2] Purple Rice, like Brown Rice, still has its bran and germ intact, so though it does have more nutrients then hulled White Rice, it also contains some anti-nutrients like phytic acid, and can be more difficult to digest if someone has weak digestion.

White Basmati Rice is one of the most easily digested foods. Along with split yellow mung beans, they are the base for our JingSmacked Kitchari (page 208). Kitchari is so easily digested and soothing for the intestines that in India it's typically given as the first food for infants.[3]

Salt

Salt is needed for the electrical function of the heartbeat, to make hydrochloric acid in the stomach, and for the fluid around the cells.[1] Salt is 40% sodium. Sodium balance is regulated in the body by aldosterone, a hormone produced by the outer adrenal cortex. People will typically have salt cravings if they have tired/fatigued adrenals. Culinarily, a little salt brings out all the other flavors in a dish. Celtic Sea Salt and Black Truffle Sea Salt are always in our JingSlinger repertoire.

Sodium Copper Chlorophyllin

Chlorophyll is a variety of green pigments in both algae and plants. It is similar in structure to human blood, with the major difference being that chlorophyll has a magnesium atom in its middle, versus an iron atom in human blood. Sodium Copper Chlorophyllin, is created from sodium salts of chlorophyll and actually has a copper atom in its center instead of magnesium. Sodium Copper Chlorophyllin has been used as a supplement since the 1940s and 1950s and topically as a deodorant and to speed wound healing.[1] It has been shown to have potent antioxidant effects, and can protect against cellular and DNA damage caused by mycotoxins produced by molds.[2]

Strawberry

Strawberries are one of nearly 3,000 species of plants that are in the rose family. Strawberries, in addition to containing minerals like manganese and iodine, nutrients like Vitamin C and folate, also contain numerous antioxidants, including 25 anthocyanins.[1]

Strawberries contain both probiotic friendly soluble fiber, as well as insoluble fiber. The insoluble fibers have been shown to be highly effective at blocking dietary mercury from being absorbed in the intestinal tract.[2]

SuperFood Shortening

This is a product from the brand Nutiva, which is an amazing upgrade for the numerous low quality vegan butter replacements that have been on the market for years. It is a blend of healthy organic saturated fats, from coconut oil and red palm oil. The red palm oil is procured from small farms and in concert with the organization Natural Habitats™, which ensures their red palm oil is not contributing to natural habitat destruction. We use this sustainable SuperFood Shortening in many baking applications. An extra bonus: it promotes the ketogenic state of fat-burning.

Sweet Potato

Sweet Potatoes were originally domesticated in Central America thousands of years ago.[1] Traditionally they are considered a fortifying food for the spleen, pancreas and kidneys.[2] Orange Sweet Potatoes gain their color, like carrots, from the antioxidant beta-carotene, and Purple Sweet Potatoes gain their color from anthocyanins.

Though Sweet Potatoes do contain a substantial amount of carbohydrates, they have been shown to actually improve insulin sensitivity, while increasing levels of adiponectin and decreasing fibrinogen.[3]

Tomato

Tomatoes are cooling in nature and have been traditionally used to cool liver heat, detox the liver, purify the blood, and build appetite.[1] Tomatoes contain a number of antioxidants, but are most famous for their high content of the beauty antioxidant lycopene. Lycopene inhibits collagenases, the enzymes which breaks down collagen.[2] Lycopene also has positive effects on the immune system and on inflammation, as it inhibits the binding of NF-kB.[3]

Turmeric Root

Perhaps the greatest of all Ayurvedic herbs and certainly one of the most widely used, Turmeric Root is a panacea of remedies.

Famous for its anti-inflammatory effects, Turmeric has been used by yogis for centuries for joint pain and flexibility. It has remarkable cleansing powers and is used for many types of situations, especially for clearing the skin, and cleaning the liver and the blood.

Turmeric's most active compounds, called curcuminoids, are fat soluble, so always consume Turmeric with some form of fat. Piperine, the active compound in black pepper, has been shown to increase absorption of curcumin by 2,000%.[1]

Vanilla Bean

Vanilla Beans are a pod that grow on the South American Vanilla Orchid and which provide the flavor for the number one most popular ice cream in the United States.

Vanilla has been known as an aphrodisiac in folk medicine and a recent study showed that just the scent of vanilla was enough to boost dopamine and serotonin levels, indicating that the scent of Vanilla could help to protect against depression.[1]

Vanillic Acid has also been shown to alleviate inflammation in a number of ways, including via the NF-Kb and COX-2 pathways.[2]

Walnuts

Walnuts not only look like a brain, they are a brain food! Used in Chinese Medicine to nourish the brain, kidneys, adrenals and the reproductive system, Walnuts have been shown to improve sperm vitality and motility.[1] They are also used traditionally to moisten the lungs and the colon.[2]

Walnuts contain the cardiovascular protective omega 3 fatty acid alpha-linolenic acid, which can be converted in small portions to the important neuro nourishing fats EPA and DHA. About 5-10% of ALA will convert to EPA and about 2-4% will convert to DHA. Walnuts also contain the neurotransmitter melatonin,[3] which is not only an antioxidant, but is the regulating signaling molecule for our sleep cycle.

Whey Protein

The protein ratio in cow's milk, the most common source of Whey Protein, is actually 80% Casein and 20% Whey. In human breast milk, the protein ratio is 40% Casein, 60% Whey.

Whey Protein contains all nine essential amino acids. It is rich in branch chain amino acids, and is the highest natural source of glutathione precursors (cysteine, glycine and glutamate). Glutathione is the most important intracellular antioxidant in the body and regulates a number of functions including cell signaling, protein function, gene expression, and cell differentiation/proliferation in the brain.[1] Whey also contains a very rare bonded form of cysteine and glutamate called glutamylcysteine, which makes glutathione production extra simple for the body. [2] Alpha-lactalbumin, one of the major proteins in whey, has been shown to boost serotonin levels, increasing cognitive performance in times of stress.[3]

People who are sensitive to either casein or lactose, will sometimes find that a Whey Protein Isolate digests the best for them, as these two elements have both been completely removed in processing. We only use Whey Protein products from grass-fed organic dairy.

Water

The quality and quantity of the water we drink is one of the most important factors in our health. Water is the "universal solvent," it is the element of youth. When we are born, our body is about 75% water, but as we age, our bodies dry out. In our elder years, our body is down to about 50% water content. Water is most concentrated in the brain, organs, and muscle tissue, along with the watery channels of blood and lymphatic fluid.

Most public drinking water in the United States is both chlorinated and medically fluoridated, so we personally avoid it as much as possible, filter it when showering, and never drink it. Chlorine is used to kill certain bacteria and other microbes in tap water and it is highly toxic.[1] Fluoride was used starting in the 1930s to medically depress overactive thyroid function.[2, 3] It is also toxic, which is why fluoridated toothpastes will contain a warning, which reads something to the effect of "Because this product contains fluoride, if more then used for brushing is swallowed, contact a poison control center immediately."

If using tap water for drinking or cooking purposes, reverse osmosis filtration should be a minimum requirement to filter both of these compounds. Additionally, tap water has been shown to contain traces of many types of prescription drug medications, which don't get completely filtered out by water treatment plants.[4, 5]

Our preferred drinking water is bottled spring water in glass with as low a TDS (total dissolved solids) as possible. Castle Rock Spring Water from Mount Shasta, California is our favorite bottled spring water on the west coast of the United States, while Raw Water from Maine is our favorite bottled spring water on the east coast.

If you are adventurous, you can hunt down your own clean (and free) spring water in your local area! If you live in North America, www.findaspring.com is a fantastic resource.

We avoid water bottled in plastic as much as possible. Water is a solvent, and plastics contain xenoestrogenic compounds that not only disrupt hormones, but that have been shown to induce transgenerational epigenetic mutations.[6] And you don't know where that plastic bottle has been! We have seen stores that display palettes of water in plastic bottles on the sidewalk, in direct sunlight, in 100°F/38°C heat!

How much water you should consume each day depends on many factors. How humid is your region of the world? How much live, watery foods do you eat, versus dry, dehydrated and packaged foods? How much do you exercise and sweat? How much do you weigh? All these things will factor in to how much water you need. Generally, 2-3 liters of water per day is the average for an adult.

The Sweet Life

Many of our clients want to keep processed sugar out of their diet. We personally have kept sugar at bay as an overall dietary principle for many years. Processed Sugar consumption leads to glycation and cross-linking in our skin (in other words, wrinkles) and a slew of other youth and health diminishing factors. For these reasons, we use primarily Stevia and Birch Xylitol for our sweeteners, so in the pages of this book, we have used these the most, but we do believe in choices!

The following are our favorite sweeteners, not all of them are included in the recipes for this book. Everyone is different and people will find that they have specific sweetener choices that they gravitate towards, so we wanted to give you a taste of our favorite options. We encourage you to play with your food!

Blackstrap Molasses

Blackstrap Molasses is the thick, mineral rich black syrup that is the byproduct (the leftovers) of the third boiling of sugarcane when making refined sugar. It is rich with minerals such as magnesium, calcium, manganese and potassium. One tablespoon of Blackstrap Molasses contains 20% of the RDA for iron. It has been used in folk medicine for numerous things, including building blood, relieving joint pain, growing hair back to its original color after greying, and as its dark black color indicates, it is a good kidney food. Blackstrap Molasses has got Jing!

Lo Han Guo

Lo Han Guo (pictured at right), more commonly known as "Monk Fruit" is a Chinese Tonic Herb, natively found in various parts of eastern Asia. It is a member of the Gourd family, and is also related to Gynostemma.[1] Though the flesh of the fruit does contain both fructose and glucose, most of its sweetness comes from its mogroside compounds, a group of terpene glycosides, which can be 300-400 times sweeter then sugar.[2] It is these mogroside extracts, which are used in the majority of Lo Han Guo products, making it an ever increasingly popular choice among people on a low sugar diet.

As a tonic herb, Lo Han Guo is used to cool, moisten and tonify the lungs and the throat. It will often be found in herbal cough syrup formulas and is also used to support the immune system in many ways.

Honey

Honey is a magical, alchemical sweetener. It is derived from the sweet nectar of flowers, which is used to attract bees to spread their pollen. The water rich nectar is pre-digested in the stomach of a bee, then passed on to multiple other bees, before being deposited in a honeycomb. Once the nectar is in the honeycomb, the bees dehydrate the water in the nectar by flapping their wings, creating the thick consistency that raw honey is known for. The stomach of a bee contains glucose oxidase enzymes, which breaks down glucose in the nectar into gluconic acid and hydrogen peroxide.[1]

Hydrogen peroxide is a very strong oxidizing and disinfectant agent[2] and is either solely, or in the case of Manuka Honey in combination with other compounds in the honey, responsible for honey's reputation for millennia as a disinfecting SuperFood. If placed in a properly sealed container, raw honey will not spoil. Honey has been found in Egyptian tombs in properly sealed containers has still been good to eat![3]

Honey should be used and consume raw. Always purchase the raw/unheated variety. In Ayurveda, raw honey builds Jing/Ojas and is used as a carrier for many herbal medicines. However, it is said in Ayurveda that when honey is heated, it will build "ama," or toxicity in the body.

Red Carpet Secret- Want to blast a cold sore? Apply Manuka Honey 20+ strength, Sovereign Silver Gel and either organic Coconut Oil or MCT Oil. The concentration and combination of these three things can knock it off course at the first tingle and shorten its appearance by days.

Honey is used in many traditions for lubricating the throat and the lungs. It has been shown to have numerous benefits, including lowering homocysteine and c-reactive protein levels.[4]

Stevia Leaf

Stevia is a green leafy shrub, indigenous to Paraguay and Brazil, though today it is grown in many different areas of the world. It is a tonic herb in Amazonian herbalism and has been used for hundreds of years as a natural sweetener. It is very popular with people on a low sugar diet or for people on an anti-candida diet because its sweetness, which comes from its glycoside content, has zero impact on blood sugar. Green Stevia Powder is between 10-40 times sweeter than regular white sugar, while Stevia's refined extracts of steviol glycosides can be up to 300 times sweeter than white sugar.

The Stevia Leaf itself, beyond being used strictly as a sweetener, has been used traditionally for lowering high blood sugar, lowering high blood pressure and used against many different types of infections.[1]

Though we do use the Green Stevia Leaf Powder in our food, for culinary reasons, we mostly use the flavored liquid Stevia Extracts. These flavored liquid extracts are processed products and may not have the same herbal benefits as the unprocessed leaf, but because they lend so much sweetness and flavor to our final nutrient dense foodie delights, we find that they are often the best culinary choice.

Some people are sensitive to the bitter aftertaste may occur with certain stevia products. This will depend a lot on the type of extraction and will also depend on a person's palate. We like to layer stevia with additional sweeteners to minimize any bitter aftertaste effect.

People who are currently taking blood pressure lowering medication or blood sugar lowering medication, should check with their doctor before using raw Stevia in large amounts because of its possible effects on these systems.

SugaVida

SugaVida is the brand name for the sweetener Palmyra Jaggery. The term "jaggery" is used in Ayurveda to describe a form of unrefined sugar, usually made from either sugarcane or from a palm tree sap. It is created in blocks (see photo below) and then powderized. There are three types of palm trees whose sap is used to make jaggery, the Coconut Palm, the Date Palm, and the "Palmyra" Palm (Borassus Flabellifer), also known as the Toddy Palm. Palmyra, far and away is the most nutritious of the three. Most importantly, the Palmyra Palm is incredibly unique because it is home to a symbiotic bacteria that actually ferments the tree sap.

Palmyra Jaggery packs an unbelievable amount nutrition. It contains minerals such as calcium, phosphorus and iron,[1] but it is the B Vitamin content of Palmyra Jaggery, which is the most impressive. One tablespoon of Palmyra Jaggery contains 600% of the RDA of Thiamin (Vitamin B1), 84% of the RDA of Riboflavin (Vitamin B2), 24% of the RDA of Niacin (Vitamin B3), 210% of the RDA of Vitamin B6 and 36% of the RDA of Vitamin B12.[2] Palmyra Jaggery may very well be the only known vegan food source of absorbable Vitamin B12 (Algae have B12 in a non-active, analogue form, that is not absorbable).[3] Palmyra Jaggery has been used in Ayurveda and has been shown in studies to act as an anti-Inflammatory.[4] It has a Glycemic Index score of 40, being 65-85% sucrose.

Culinarily, Palmyra Jaggery is tremendous. We use it in a similar way as we do black truffle salt, and foods that provide a savory "umami" flavor, only we use Palmyra with its sweet flavor and undertones, adding additional depths of flavor to our food. It is one of our favorite JingSlinger kitchen secrets for both sweet and savory dishes!

Maple Syrup

Maple Syrup is a 40:1 concentrate of maple sap, in which most of the water has been boiled out of it. It has been consumed for hundreds of years, originally by the Native Americans in North America. Most of the world's supply is produced in Canada, as well as in the United States in Vermont, New York and Maine.

Maple Syrup is rich in a variety of antioxidants and trace minerals, though not enough to be a significant dietary source of any of them. It is relatively high in sugar (13 grams per tablespoon), mostly of sucrose. Because it is an actual sugar, it may not be appropriate for people who are diabetic, pre-diabetic or have candida issues. It is sometimes argued that because Maple Syrup is not a significant source of any one nutrient that it is not worth the sugar consumption. We like to keep this quote in mind from one study on its antioxidant content, which should always be considered with all whole foods:

"In view of the well-established antioxidant activity these substances (maple syrup grades) possess, it is suggested that it is the complexity of the mixture rather than any one compound that may serve to counter the unhealthful presence of the high concentration of sugars in the syrup."[1]

Maple syrup has wonderful culinary applications and in Canada, and areas where it is harvested and consumed heavily, it is used liberally on both sweet and savory dishes.

Birch Xylitol

Xylitol is a polyalcohol, or "sugar alcohol," (a five carbon sugar, as opposed to regular sugar which has six carbons) which is found in many fruits and vegetables. The human body produces between 5-15 grams of Xylitol per day via normal metabolism.[1] It was first discovered in the 1890s in Europe and rose to popularity as a sweetener in Europe during World War II sugar shortages.

Because of it's structure, a large percentage of Xylitol is not digested, and it has very minimum effects on blood sugar, with a Glycemic Index count of 8 and a Glycemic Load count of only 1. It is becoming more and more popular for people on a low sugar diet, and also for people on an anti-candida diet, as it has been shown to significantly lower acetaldehyde, a toxic byproduct of candida.[2] Xylitol has also been shown to remineralize the deeper layers of demineralized tooth enamel by facilitating calcium movement in the teeth.[3]

As with other sugar alcohols (Erythritol, Maltitol, Mannitol, Sorbitol) Xylitol can cause some stomach sensitivity (gas, bloating, diarrhea) in some people, particularly in large doses, so if you are new to it, introduce it slowly, starting with 1-2 teaspoons to test it out. Anecdotally, we have found that a person's tolerance to Xylitol, even if sensitive at first, can build up quite rapidly, especially the cleaner and stronger their digestive tract becomes.

Today, Xylitol is derived mainly from corn cobs, so some of it on the market is sourced from GMO-corn. We personally only use the Xylitol derived from hardwood sources. If it is derived from a hardwood source, it will always be stated on the package. Xylitol is NOT to be consumed by pets. Like chocolate, grapes and many other foods, it is harmful to dogs and cats, because they can not metabolize it the way humans do. For more on using Xylitol culinarily, see page 69.

Beyond the Plate...

"The Power of Powders"

This *"Beyond the Plate"* segment is both a time-saver and is also lightening fast *JingSlinger Alchemy* on the fly. We want you to bring nutrient density to everything you eat, from your *Morning Smoothies* to your *Moma's Marinara* with these SuperFood powders. Just pick how you want to feel and *Sling Away*! Follow our lead in the recipes we have perfected so you can learn *to lean into the flavors* and therefore know what herbs work best with what you are creating, so you can have both function and flavor!

Awaken the Shen™

This is an amazing formula from the company Jing Herbs of over a dozen Chinese Tonic Herbs, designed to calm, balance the emotions and open the heart.

It contains herbs such as Reishi Mushroom, Albizzia Flower, Asparagus Root, Polygala Root, Pearl Powder, Longan Berry, He Shou Wu, Schizandra Berry, and many more.

This is one of the stars of our nighttime "Sleeping BeauTea" elixir (page 157).

How do you want to feel?

Arnox™ Advantage

Arnox™ Advantage is a brand name product from Anova Health. It is an L-Arginine and L-Citrulline based product with a number of food and herbal concentrates, all designed to nourish and tonify the endothelium of the blood vessels and support production of nitric oxide.

Nitric oxide is a powerful signaling molecule, which has numerous functions in the body. It was named "Molecule of the Year" in 1992 (who knew there was a such a thing!). It is the signaling molecule for vasodilation and is critical for blood flow throughout the body. The 1998 Nobel Prize in Medicine was awarded to three researchers for their decades of study into Nitric Oxide's effects as a signaling molecule in the cardiovascular system.

In folk medicine from around the world, when you look at the top herbs that have been used for cardiovascular support, whether it is Hawthorn Berry in North American herbalism, Salvia Root in Chinese Herbalism, or Arjuna Bark in Ayurvedic herbalism, they all boost Nitric Oxide in the body.

Arnox™ Advantage is sweetened with Lo Han Guo, Xylitol and Stevia, so it has very minimum effect on blood sugar, yet tastes like sweet fruit punch.

Blue Majik™

This is a blue pigment phycocyanin concentrate from Spirulina, a type of blue-green algae. It is used as an outstanding natural anti-inflammatory as it has been shown to lower the COX-2 pathway of inflammation[1]. It has antioxidant effects and can increase the expression of certain antioxidant enzymes and enzymes systems, such as cytochrome P450, superoxide dismutase, and catalase[2]. E3Live Blue Majik™ smells strongly like fish food but it plays remarkably nice on the palate when mixed in certain recipes with the right other SuperFoods. You won't even know it's in there!

Restore the Jing™

When we're Slinging it in the kitchen and we want to Jing Up one of our recipes, this is our go-to powder. It is a formula of eight Chinese Tonic Herbs from the company Jing Herbs and features several major Jing boosting tonic herbs such as Morinda Root, Eucommia Bark, and Prepared Rehmannia Root.

Miracle Reds™

Miracle Reds is a raw powdered SuperFood formula containing over 40 nutrient rich food concentrates, herbal extracts and probiotics from the company MacroLife. It easily integrates into berry flavored recipes, and is a fantastic SuperFood formula for children. It is also easy to find, nearly any Whole Foods Market or health food store will carry it.

Brain On®

E3Live Brain On® is a phycocyanin (see "Blue Majik") and phenylethylamine (PEA) concentrate. The PEA is derived from a blue-green algae called Aphanizomenon Flos-Aquae (AFA). PEA is known as the "Love Molecule," it is the same compound that is found in chocolate that enhances our brain and opens our heart. PEA boosts and protects a number of important neurotransmitters including dopamine, norepinephrine, acetylcholine and serotonin[1], which means that not only can it help to give you more "get up and go" in your everyday, it can also boost libido AND help you find your keys!

Pure Radiance™

Unlike most other animals, the bodies of certain primates, including humans, cannot synthesize their own Vitamin C due to a genetic mutation on the L-gulono-γ-lactone oxidase (*GLO*) gene[1], and so we must obtain in our diet. Pure Radiance is a food-derived Vitamin C concentrate from some of the highest food sources from around the world, including camu berry, amla berry, acerola berry, rose hips and lemon peel. It has a sour taste and works well with lemon/lime or fruity recipes.

Pure Synergy™

Demonstrating the power of powders, Pure Synergy is a powered mix of 60 different organic SuperFoods. It contains a wide spectrum of algae, enzymes, grasses, sprouts, tonic herbs and medicinal mushrooms. In the early days of the Erewhon Tonic Bar, Pure Synergy was known as "The Bar in a Jar" because people could get a little bit of everything from behind the bar, with just one formula.

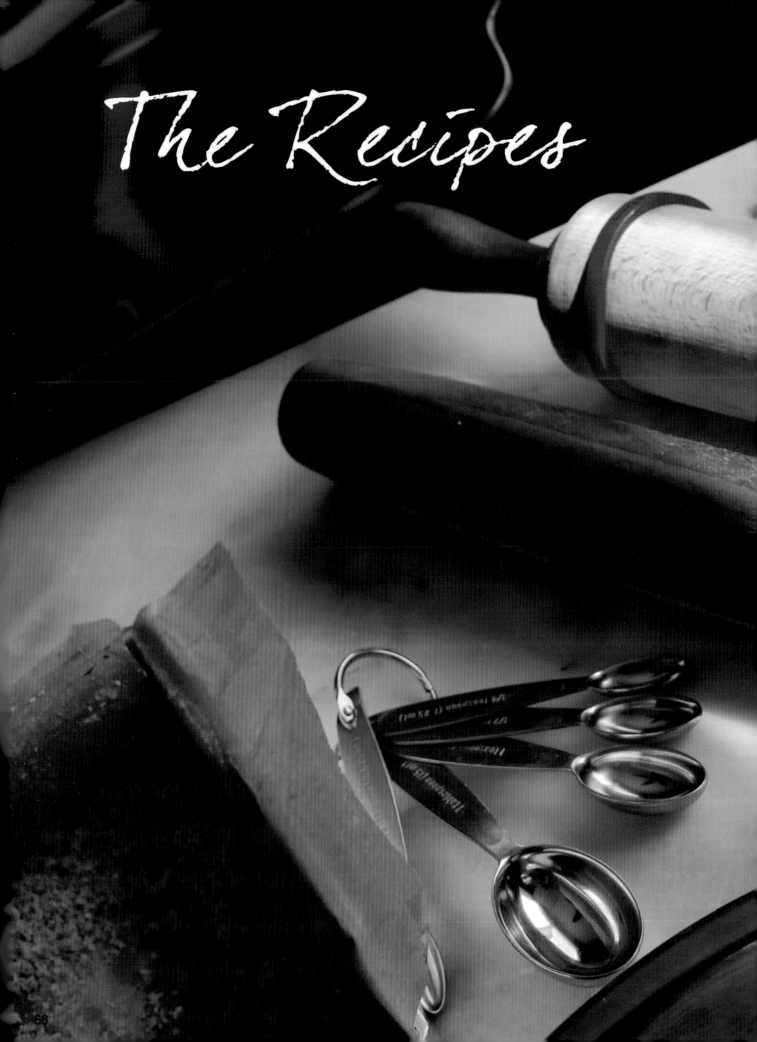

The Recipes

Stuff You Should Know!

With one more flip of the page, you will be swan diving headfirst into our Clever Comfort Food Recipes.

But first, for the sake of simplicity, we have compiled some S.Y.S.K. (Stuff You Should Know) about our recipes and about using this cookbook. This is a section about simplicity, so that's all we are saying for an intro, here's some S.Y.S.K.!

- We have recipes within recipes! Because "Everyone is Welcome at Our Table," we have taken the time to adapt our recipes for many different diets, so the Paleo version of a recipe may be on one page, while the Vegan version is on the facing page, or maybe the base recipe is Vegan and then we explain in a highlighted section how to Sling it Paleo with optional ingredients. Many of our recipes will work for all diets across the board. Also, we have recipes in this book that you can flip into dozens of different things and a myriad of different flavors. We encourage you to play with your food... brilliantly.

- Whenever we refer to any kind of food throughout this book, we are always speaking about organic and Non-GMO. When we thought about how much space it was going to take to write "organic" in front of every single food item, we knew there had to be a simple way of doing it. So for the record, everything is organic, whenever there is such a thing. In this cookbook organic is the norm, so we don't have to actually label it.

- All animal foods are from Organic, Pasture Raised animals who have been fed their natural diet. For cows, that's grass, for chickens, it's bugs and other roaming critters. This is again for simplicity's sake, we're saving a lot of ink by not saying "free roaming, grass finished, antibiotic free, etc." in front of every animal product in every recipe, just know that they are.

- "Water" is always ideally Spring Water or well-filtered Water like Reverse Osmosis. If you read the section on Water (page 56), you'll know why we don't touch the medically treated, antibiotic water that comes out of most city sources. So good, clean Spring Water is just referred to as "Water" from now on.

- "Coconut Milk" always means **Full-Fat** Coconut Milk, unless specifically noted, which does happen once or twice. We're talking about the Full Fat Coconut Milk that comes in small bottles, or in the BPA free cans. We're not talking about the kind in the larger boxes, those are too diluted, and usually contain a lot of synthetic vitamins and preservatives. This isn't the 1980s, so we're using Full-Fat here.

- We did our best to eliminate brand names as much as possible, some of the products we use are actually a trademarked name and sometimes a specific product from a specific brand is crucial for a recipe to turn out in that over-the-top delicious way that we want all of your recipes to turn out.

Having said that, here are some of the brands that we use regularly, and why:

- The flavored Stevias we refer to throughout the book, unless specifically noted, are the Sweetleaf brand. This makes a difference culinarily for consistent flavor.

- Our favorite MCT Oil is Bulletproof Brain Octane Oil (page 36). We use the Bulletproof product line whenever possible because of their quality standards.

- The Ghee (page 44) we use and have been using for years is the Ancient Organics brand. It makes all the difference with its buttery-toffee flavor. It does not need to be refrigerated. Ghee will only go bad if it becomes contaminated with bacteria from a dirty spoon, or if taken in and out of refrigeration repeatedly and condensation forms inside the bottle. Leave your Ghee at room temperature.

- The "SuperFood Shortening" (page 53) we use in our recipes is from the company Nutiva. It is important for both consistency and flavor.

We use both whey protein and collagen powder in a lot of our recipes for added protein. If you want to use a Vegan protein substitute, choose one that has a light, creamy flavor so it mixes well culinarily. There are a number of Vegan protein powders on the market that match this description, so just use your favorite one wherever we use the term "Vanilla Vegan Protein."

- If a recipe calls for Xylitol Powder, but all you have is Xylitol Crystals, then grind them in a clean coffee grinder or in a high performance blender, they will powderize easily! If you want to take it one step further, you can sift the powder to get out any remaining crystals or clumps (for more about Xylitol, see page 61).

- The "Jing It Up" section of our recipes are always ADDITIONAL OPTIONS. Choose one, none, or all of them! It's up to you! Some people work with lots of SuperFoods and Tonic Herbs, some people are just getting started with them, so no worries! The "Jing It Up" options are not required for the recipe. If it's necessary, it is in the "Gather Up" portion of the recipe.

- A couple notes on Gluten-Free baking, just FYI... Gluten-Free Flour is more "thirsty" then regular flour, so we use a little extra liquid and oil to balance them. Because they are so thirsty, you cannot just readily swap Butter (water content) out for Ghee (no water content) in our GF recipes. Make sense? Also, Gluten-Free Flours require a slightly higher oven temperature to bake correctly, which we have factored in, so just be aware of that if you are used to baking with conventional flour.

Measurement Abbreviations we use throughout this book:
Teaspoon(s): tsp
Tablespoon(s): TB
Milliliter(s): ml
Gram(s): g
Ounce(s): oz

That's it! Aprons on! Time to Sling!

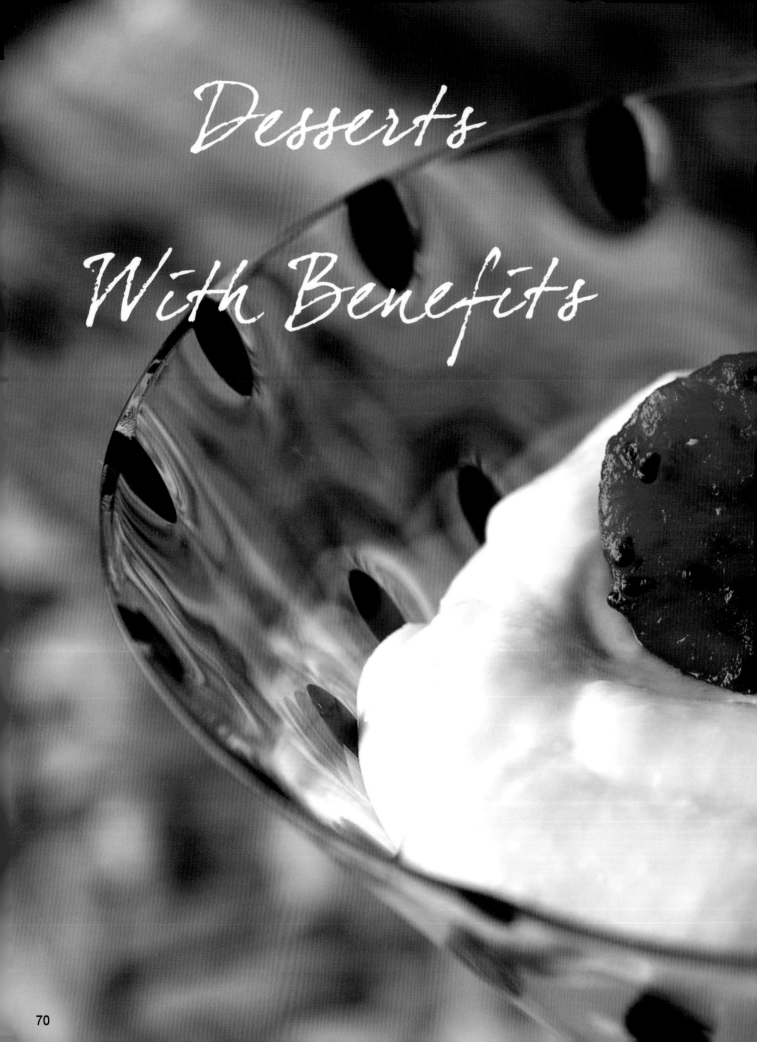

Desserts With Benefits

"Life is short,
eat dessert first." Jacques Torres

Over the Top...

Sauces, Fillings & Toppings... Oh My!

Whipped Cream 101

Lauric, capric and caprylic fatty acids never tasted so good! Heart healthy, brain boosting and fat burning, Whipped Cream is back on the menu! You can create this Coconut Whipped Cream in a stand mixer, with an electric hand mixer or an immersion blender. Creating flavored Whipped Creams becomes limitless with flavored liquid stevia, organic extracts, essential oils, powderized freeze-dried fruit and herbs... and don't forget cacao powder, Chocolate Whipped Cream is a heavenly ketogenic treat! Want a Raspberry Cream? Simply whirl the freeze dried fruit in your clean spice or coffee grinder until it is a fine powder, stop the mixer and sift the powder into the cream in the last few minutes of whipping, then continue whipping until fully incorporated. Chef Note - All powders should be sifted to create a smooth flavored Whipped Cream.

Gather Up

2 cups (500ml) Coconut Cream (from 2 cans of Coconut Milk, chilled in refrigerator overnight)
½ tsp Vanilla Stevia
½ tsp Pearl Powder (optional)

Jing It Up (choose one)

2-3 TB powderized/sifted freeze dried Fruit of choice
2-3 TB Cacao Powder, sifted
1 TB Arnox Advantage

For Wildberry Cream - 1 tsp Miracle Reds, 2 TB Raspberry Powder, with 1 TB Blueberry Powder

Sling it up

Without shaking the cans of chilled coconut milk, carefully open them, and scoop out just the coconut cream, collected from the top of the can. Save the remaining coconut water for future recipes or to thin your coconut cream while whisking, if needed.

With the whisk attached, place coconut cream into the bowl of your stand mixer. Beat on high speed. Add the vanilla stevia, pearl powder and any additional flavors or powder you wish to infuse (a teaspoon at a time) after about 3 minutes, by stopping the mixer, scraping down the sides and adding additional sweetener to balance the powders you have chosen. It is ready once the coconut cream has expanded in volume, and makes "stiff peaks."

If the coconut cream has not increased in volume after about 4 minutes of whisking, then add 1 teaspoon at a time of the remaining coconut water to get a lighter consistency that will whip up and expand. However, know that too much coconut water will make it too thin and no "Whip Cream" will form.

Transfer to a piping bag, or store in an airtight container in the refrigerator for up to a week.

SuperFood Salted Caramel

It's a bird... It's a plane... It's SuperFood Salted Caramel! This sauce embodies one of our JingSlinger taste profile principles: It's even better than the real thing! It is loaded with hormone building beneficial fat, infused with SuperFoods and Tonic Herbs. The brand of the base ingredient is imperative in this formula, it has to be Ancient Organics Ghee for the right buttery, toffee taste, and the Vegan version needs to be the Nutiva SuperFood Shortening. Ice with it, dip in it, spread it... SuperFood Salted Caramel has an infinite number of applications, sweet or savory. We're even showing you how to flip it into our Salted Caramel Quinoa Crunchies! *How do you like them (salted caramel) apples?!*

Gather up

1 cup (225g) Ghee or SuperFood Shortening
⅔ cup (135g) Xylitol Powder, sifted
⅔ cup (85g) Lucuma Powder
2 TB Sunflower Lecithin Powder

2 TB Maca Powder
1½ tsp Toffee Stevia
1 teaspoon Sea Salt
⅛ teaspoon Cinnamon Powder
2 cups (160g) Puffed Quinoa (if making Crunchies)

Sling It Up

Use a double boiler or simply fit a heatproof metal bowl over a medium saucepan containing two inches of water. Bring the water to a simmer, then turn it down to low heat. Melt the ghee/superfood shortening in the metal bowl until it is liquid. Add in your ingredients one by one while stirring continuously. Xylitol powder needs to be put through a sifter to remove any gritty crystals. Add the sea salt last.

Once fully mixed, transfer to a heatproof container such as a large glass Pyrex liquid measuring cup. (If you are using it right away, to top or stir into a JingLato, it is ready to eat!)

If you are not using it right away, or you are making Salted Caramel Quinoa Crunchies, set a timer and stir briskly with a large fork once every five minutes to ensure that the oil remains incorporated while cooling and does not separate. Do this 3-4 times, over 15-20 minutes. Next, repeat the stirring process two more times, while having it in the refrigerator to cool more rapidly for 10 additional minutes. Once completely cooled, transfer to an airtight glass container. It can be stored at room temperature and will last several weeks.

To make Salted Caramel Quinoa Crunchies, you want the mixture to be a little warm, and the consistency to be easy to stir. Depending on the temperature in your kitchen, this should occur after the initial 15-20 minute cooling period, and may need 5 minutes in the refrigerator to thicken a bit.

If your Pyrex container is large enough, simply pour the Puffed Quinoa into the Salted Caramel Sauce and stir the mixture very well, making sure the Puffed Quinoa is evenly incorporated.

Fill your favorite mini silicon molds. Put them in the freezer to set and in about one hour, you will have Salted Caramel Quinoa Crunchies! They can be stored in either the refrigerator or in the freezer. They can be eaten straight out of cold storage, or left at room temperature for 5 minutes to soften just before eating.

Lemon Curd

The Vegan Lemon Curd is excellent for icing and filling cupcakes, tarts and cookies. The Paleo Lemon Curd rocks our JingSlinger Shortbread Crust (page 132) into an amazing Lemon Meringue Pie. These versatile Lemon Curds look mild mannered, but pack a nutritional punch and a variety of beneficial fats. The bioflavonoids in the fresh zest, rutin and quercetin, are important antioxidant avengers for improved blood flow and capillary integrity. They also support elastin and collagen, to help you Get Your Glow On!

Gather up (Vegan)

1 cup (150g) Raw Cashews (not soaked)
6 TB (84g) SuperFood Shortening
5 TB (75ml) Lemon Juice
3 TB Coconut Milk
2 TB Xylitol Powder
3 TB Lucuma Powder
1 TB packed fine Lemon Zest
1 tsp SunFlower Lecithin Powder
⅛ tsp Turmeric Powder

Gather Up (Paleo)

6 Egg Yolks, separated, save the whites for another recipe
1 cup (200g) Xylitol Powder
½ cup (110g) Ghee, chilled
½ cup (120ml) fresh squeezed Lemon Juice
3 TB fresh Lemon Zest

Jing It Up (Vegan)

¼ tsp Pure Radiance or Camu Powder
½ tsp MCT Oil

Jing It Up (Paleo)

¼ tsp Pure Radiance
½ tsp Pearl Powder
½ tsp MCT Oil

Sling It Up (Vegan)

Place all of the Vegan lemon curd ingredients into the blender and blast until smooth. You can add a tablespoon of filtered water a bit at a time if the mixture is too chunky and doesn't blend smooth. Chill in the fridge in a covered dish until it is a spreadable cream. Fill or top our raw Praline Cookies (page 118) for our Lemoncello Pralindo Cookies made in minutes, no oven!

Sling It Up (Paleo)

Bring one inch of water to a simmer over medium heat in a medium size saucepan. Place a medium size heatproof metal bowl on top of the saucepan, without touching the water. In this bowl, whisk together the egg yolks and xylitol powder until smooth. Add the lemon juice, lemon zest and Pure Radiance to the mixture and continue to whisk. Whisk until well blended and until it thickens (approximately 6-8 minutes). Remove from heat and stir in 1 tablespoon of the chilled ghee at a time, until it is fully incorporated, before adding the next tablespoon. Add all the ghee in this manner. Taste the lemon curd for sweetness and add additional vanilla stevia if necessary.

Transfer to a sealed glass container and refrigerate for up to 7-10 days. It also freezes well.

Jing Jam

Gather up

3 cups (750ml) Pomegranate Juice
½ cup (80g) Chia Seeds
1½ cups (345g) Raspberries (frozen or fresh)
1-2 TB Xylitol (to taste)
½ tsp Vanilla Stevia

Jing It Up

1 tsp Freeze-Dried Acai Powder
1 tsp Freeze-Dried Maqui Powder
2 tsp Miracle Reds Powder
2 tsp Arnox Advantage

Sling it up

Add everything except the berries into the pomegranate juice. Stir and allow to thicken, about 15 minutes.

Throw just the frozen berries in the blender and "pulse" a few times to rough cut all the berries. Fresh berries can simply be muddled with a fork.

Stir the berries into the Jing Jam mixture. Refrigerate and layer in a glass with coconut whipped cream for an instant superfood trifle.

Orange Marvelade

Gather up

2½ cups (620ml) Fresh Squeezed
Orange or Tangerine Juice
½ cup (80g) Chia Seeds
¼ cup (25g) Orange Peel, thinly shaved
½ cup (112g) Orange Segments, peeled,
seeded & membrane removed
2 TB Orange Zest, fine
1-2 TB Xylitol (to taste)
½ tsp Vanilla Stevia
¼ tsp Orange Cream Stevia

Jing It Up

½ tsp Pure Radiance
½ tsp Camu Powder
1 tsp Pearl Powder

Sling it up

Simply use a potato peeler to shave the orange peel
in the correct thickness. A fine zester or microplane
can be used to produce the orange zest needed. In
a medium bowl add the chia seeds, zest and xylitol
into the juice, stir and set aside to thicken, about
15 minutes. Once thickened (for a smooth, no seed
Marvelade) add everything, except the shaved
orange peel into the blender including any Jing It Up
options, and pulse until smooth. Taste the blended
mixture and adjust the sweetness with additional
xylitol if needed

Stir in the shaved orange peels and allow to set in
the fridge (for about 30 minutes) before using.

JingSlinger Chocolate Sauce

Heirloom chocolate, the "Food of the Gods," is loaded with a staggering array of nutrients and feel-good complex compounds. This ain't your dime-store chocolate! This recipe is the glaze for our Epic Éclairs (page 130), it is the chocolate shell and ripples in our JingLatos (page 100), it is what our SlingShots (page 126) prefer to be dressed in... there are so many uses for this one recipe throughout this cookbook!

Cacao beans are stacked with cell supporting minerals such as calcium, chromium, iron, magnesium, and zinc, as well as many different types of antioxidants. It is jam-packed with neurotransmitters such as PEA and anandamide, which is known as the "bliss chemical." Cacao also brings tryptophan to the table, a precursor to serotonin. Cacao contains several vasodilators, making it one of our favorite ingredients for combining with additional SuperFoods and Tonic Herbs for better delivery.

Gather Up

1 cup (125g) Cacao Powder, sifted
¼ cup (60ml) Coconut Oil, melted
¼ cup (60ml) Cacao Butter, melted

½ cup (200g) Xylitol Powder, sifted
½ tsp Vanilla Stevia
½ tsp Chocolate Stevia

Jing It Up

1 tsp He Shou Wu
1 tsp Pearl Powder
1 tsp Restore the Jing

Sling It Up

Over a medium saucepan containing about two inches of water, simply fit a heatproof metal bowl on top, so that the bottom of the bowl is not touching the water. Bring the water to a simmer, then turn it down to low heat. Add the coconut oil and cacao butter to the bowl and stir once they are liquid. Add the stevias and stir well. Add the sifted cacao powder and xylitol powder, stirring until well incorporated. Sprinkle in your Jing It Up options, while stirring. Taste the chocolate and if you would like it sweeter, add additional sifted xylitol powder, one tablespoon at a time until it reaches your desired sweetness.

Chic Cheat - Quick & Easy Melted Chocolate Glaze

Melt 9oz (255g) of Lily's Sugar-Free Chocolate chips (or a Lily's Chocolate Bar roughly chopped) along with a teaspoon of MCT oil or a teaspoon of ghee in a heatproof bowl over two inches of simmering water in a medium size pan (so that the water does not touch the bottom of the bowl). This is an instant chocolate shell, just looking for ice cream! Or mix with an equal amount of puffed quinoa and spoon into silicone molds, as pictured and refrigerate for a crunchy chocolate treat and cupcake accessory (page 112).

Vanilla Bean Chia Pudding

with Saigon Cinnamon

Wanna Spoon?

Puddings, Panna Cotta & Cannoli

Pure Green Joy Key Lime Love

This crave-worthy pudding is a lustrous hair, skin and nails bonanza! It is an alkalizing, hydrating, macronutrient powerhouse, which is one of our many "eat it anytime of the day" desserts.

It is blender biohacking at its best, especially when you Jing It Up!

Gather Up

2 large Avocados, peeled and pitted

½ cup (120ml) Coconut Milk

¼ cup (110g) Coconut Oil

½ cup (120ml) Lemon or Lime Juice

1 TB Lemon or Lime Zest (packed firm)

2 TB Sunflower Lecithin Powder (optional)

½ cup (100g) Xylitol Powder (or to taste)

1 tsp Vanilla Stevia

⅛ tsp Sea Salt

2 TB Collagen Powder (Paleo option)

1-2 TB of Ghee or SuperFood Shortening

1 tsp Chloroxygen Chlorophyll

Jing It Up

2 tsp Pearl Powder

1 tsp Pure Radiance

2 tsp Pure Synergy

Sling It Up

Place everything into the blender and blend on high speed until smooth and fully incorporated. Taste it and tweak the sweetness if necessary. Spoon into cups and chill for about an hour or pour into a JingSlinger sugar-free, grain-free, gluten-free Shortbread Crust (page 132) and chill. Serve with dollops of Coconut Whipped Cream (page 74) and/or puffed quinoa.

Bravocado

Bravocado and BuckShot are two of our original JingSlinger 1-bowl, 1-spoon recipes. Bravocado, however, transforms from fudge to "Epic Icing" if it is mixed in a food processor with additional sweetness from a bit more xylitol powder, to taste. Plus you can use it as a facial masque! (page 210).

This baby doesn't love a high performance blender, because the heat created by the blades accentuates the avocado flavor and puts the chocolate into a supporting role. Hand mixing old-school with a wooden spoon and bowl works great, but a food processor saves both time and elbow grease.

Rich in oleic acid, a healthy omega-9 fatty acid, Bravocado provides a crucial building block for your myelin, the protective sheath around your nerve network. Not bad for a cupcake... Cupcake!

Gather Up

2 cups (425g) (packed) Fresh Avocado, peeled and pitted
¾ cup (95g) Cacao Powder
½ cup (110g) Cacao Butter, melted and room temperature
¼ cup (60g) Coconut Oil, melted and room temperature
¼ cup (60ml) Coconut Cream (see page 74)
1 ¼ cup (285g) Xylitol Powder*
2 TB Sunflower Lecithin Powder
½ tsp Vanilla Stevia (or more to taste)
1 tsp Chocolate Stevia
½ cup Tera's Vanilla Whey Powder, Collagen Powder, or Vegan Vanilla Protein Powder

*If using a protein powder that is already sweetened, use ½ cup of xylitol powder until the Bravocado is blended smooth and taste for level of sweetness. Add the remaining ½ cup of xylitol powder in increments of two tablespoons at a time, until you hit your perfect sweet spot.

Sling It Up

Place all ingredients into your food processor except the melted cacao butter and melted coconut oil. While the Bravocado is spinning, pour the melted oils in a steady stream, until fully incorporated. The consistency should be like a thick pudding, or even thicker, like an icing.

Transfer the Bravocado into a piping bag to use as an icing and chill in the refrigerator to keep it firm. To use as a pudding or as a cake filling, store in an airtight container. It will last 4-7 days in the refrigerator, if it becomes too stiff to pipe simply leave at room temperature for 10-15 minutes and check it. The warmth of your hands through the pastry bag will soften it as well.

Jing It Up

1 tsp Astragalus Powder
1 tsp He Shou Wu Powder
1 tsp Restore the Jing
½ tsp Deer Antler Extract
1 tsp MCT Oil

Nutrient dense enough to be a meal on the go, yet delicious enough to be dessert. This vanilla frosting can be eaten as a power-packed snack, or can be used as a kick-ass icing and also a cream filling on pretty much anything.

BuckShot

Gather up

¼ cup (30g) Colostrum Powder
¼ cup (85g) Ghee
2 TB Whey Protein Powder
¼ tsp Vanilla Stevia
1 tsp Birch Xylitol Powder
OR
1 TB Organic Raw Honey
A pinch of Sea Salt

Jing It Up

1 TB Collagen Powder (optional)
½ tsp Deer Antler
1 tsp Pearl Powder
A pinch of Sea Salt

Sling it up

Mix all ingredients in a small bowl, stirring well until fully incorporated and smooth. The ghee should be soft, if your ghee is hard at room temperature, you can soften it by simply stirring it and creaming it into the powders vigorously... a little kitchen Cross-Fit for your forearms. If your whey powder is already sweetened, then adjust your sweeteners of choice accordingly. This recipe doesn't need to be refrigerated because ghee is stable at room temperature. BuckShot travels beautifully in a sealed container for days.

Vegan icing doesn't have the same anabolic bang of the Paleo version BUT here is the swap out -
1 cup raw Thai Coconut Meat, ⅓ cup SuperFood Shortening, ¼ cup Coconut Milk, ¼ cup Xylitol Powder, 2 TB of your favorite Vanilla Protein Powder, Vanilla Stevia to taste. Blend the coconut meat and milk in your food processor and add the remaining ingredients blending until icing smooth.

Holy Cannoli !

This is both a Vegan and Paleo probiotic dessert delight! Traditional Italian flavor and mouth feel, with fat-burning secret weapons and skin support for amazing luminosity. Additional bonus – this is a 1-bowl, 1-spoon recipe. Our clever 100% coconut wrap shell can be made using simple metal cannoli forms (see picture insert), which you can buy at any cake decorating store or baking supply store. These can be whipped up in 30 minutes or less!

Gather up

Cannoli Filling

16 oz (450 g) Kite Hill Ricotta Almond Cheese
½ tsp Vanilla Extract
¼ tsp Almond Extract
¾ cup (150g) Birch Xylitol Powder, to taste
3 TB Coconut Cream (page 74)
½ tsp Vanilla Stevia (or more to taste)
¼ cup (50g) Lilly's Sugar-Free Chocolate Chips

Cannoli Shell

One package Coconut Paleo Wraps
(7 wraps per bag)
¼ cup (50 g) Lilly's Sugar-Free Chocolate Chips, melted double boiler style (page 82)
Chopped raw Pistachio (optional)

Jing It Up

2 tsp Pearl Powder
1 tsp MCT Oil
⅛ tsp Vanilla Bean Powder

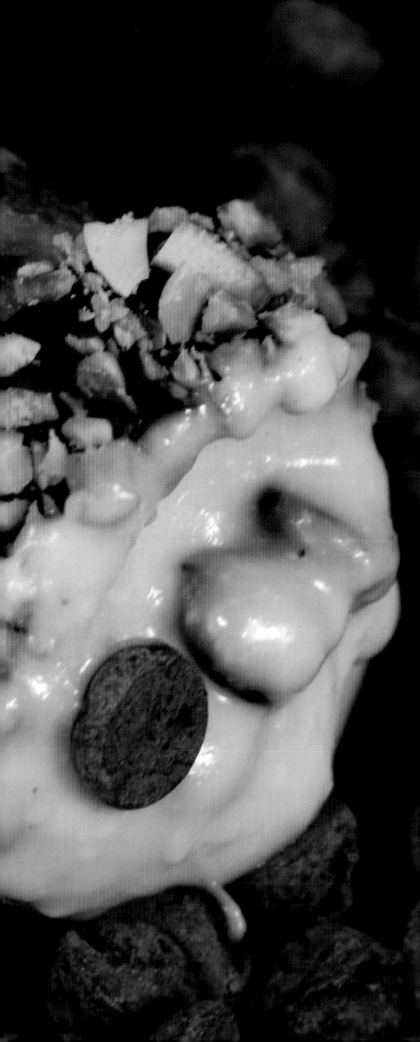

Sling it up

Add all of the filling Ingredients into a large bowl, except for the chocolate chips, and stir until well combined. Taste for sweetness and adjust accordingly. Add the chocolate chips, stir until evenly distributed. Place the filling in a piping bag, fitted with a large round tip (or in a plastic baggie with one of the corners cut off to create a make-shift piping bag). Refrigerate while making the shells to firm up.

To use the metal cannoli forms, simply fold the Paleo Wraps "point-to-point," as shown in picture insert. Tightly roll the wrap onto the cannoli form, moistening the final pointed edge with a little bit of water to seal the seam. Lay the wrapped forms on a parchment lined baking sheet with the seam side down.

Place in a 350°F/177°C oven, turning them once or twice, so that they brown evenly on all sides. You are going to have to watch them carefully, they brown up quickly! The entire baking process can take less then 3-4 minutes, depending on your oven.

Take the shells out to cool. Once cooled, slip them off the forms and dip each open end in the melted chocolate and sprinkle with chopped pistachios. Chill them in the fridge on the same parchment lined pan.

Always fill the cannoli shells just before serving (so that they do not get soggy) using the piping bag. If you wish, dust them with xylitol powder for a great presentation.

Coconut Crème Brûlée Divinity

Our Rock Star approved buttery Crème Brûlée infused with fragrant raw vanilla bean and spun from coconut meat, coconut cream, coconut oil, and coconut milk is the perfect nosh any time of the day. It is extremely hydrating, assists with rejuvenating oxidative tissue damage and supports the function of our nervous system. The concentrated MCT oil helps burn fat and fuels your brain while the caprylic, capric and lauric acid properties are antimicrobial, antifungal and antibacterial so your immune system gets some love too... Oh... and it is flippin' delicious.

Gather up

2 cups (454g) Raw Young Thai Coconut Meat (page 158)
½ cup (120ml) Coconut Cream (see page 74)
⅓ cup (75ml) Coconut Milk
1 TB of Coconut Oil
½ cup Xylitol Powder
2 TB Sunflower Lecithin Powder
¼ tsp Vanilla Bean Powder
½ tsp Vanilla Extract
1 tsp Vanilla Stevia
¼ tsp Sea Salt

Jing It Up

2 tsp Pearl Powder
1-2 TB Ghee
1 TB MCT Oil
1 TB Collagen Powder

Sling It Up

If you do not have a high performance blender simply process all of the ingredients in your food processor and then transfer it to your blender to blend until smooth. This recipe can be prepared with a food processor only, however the texture will not be the silky smooth Crème Brûlée we love to serve. This Crème Brûlée can be served in small ramekins topped with our JingSlinger Chocolate Sauce (page 82) and chilled. It can also be spooned into either one of our Pie Crusts (page 132), dressed with sliced fresh bananas or layered with berries and then crowned with Chocolate Whipped Cream (page 74) and toasted coconut flakes for our "Pie's The Limit!"

Chia Pudding 101

Famous because of the Chia Pet craze of the 1980s, chia seed became famous as a SuperFood when it was written about as a staple in the diet of the Tarahumara Native Americans, the greatest ultra distance runners in the world, in the 2009 New York Times Bestselling Book "Born to Run." As the name suggests, "Chi-a" (Chi/Qi) is a high-energy and endurance food. It is very hydrophilic, it's loaded with soluble fiber, which gelatinizes in liquid. Gelatinize some chia seed, add some protein, some fat and you're good to go. Add some additional SuperFoods and Tonic Herbs, and you are WAY good!

When gelatinizing chia seed, your liquid should to be at least room temperature. Cold liquids do not work well. When using most protein powders, or a polyunsaturated fat like Styrian pumpkin seed oil, keep the temperature down below 120°F/49°C. If you are using collagen powder and saturated fats with high heat tolerances, you can make a hot Chia Pudding, which is excellent in the winter months.

Below we have a Vanilla Chia Pudding. Enjoy it as is, or get creative, use it as a base and Sling it any number of flavors, such as with our super green food VelociTea.

Gather Up

1 cup (250ml) Coconut Milk
½ cup (120ml) Water
¼ cup (50g) Chia Seeds
2 TB Whey Protein/ Vanilla Vegan Protein
½ tsp Vanilla Stevia
1 tsp Xylitol Powder (or more to taste)

Jing It Up

1 tsp Pearl Powder
½ tsp Vanilla Bean Powder
1 tsp – 1 TB MCT Oil
1 TB Ghee/ Coconut Oil
2 TB Colostrum Powder

VelociTea Chia Pudding

1 TB Barley Grass Powder
½ tsp Matcha Extract
¼ tsp ChlorOxygen Chlorophyll
1 TB Stryrian Pumpkin Seed Oil
½ tsp E3Live Blue Majik™
2 tsp SugaVida

All of the SuperFood options for this pudding are powerful on their own, so when you combine them, look out! Barley grass powder is one of the most nutritious SuperFood powders in the world, and has a mellow, creamy flavor. It is rich in antioxidants such as superoxide dismutase (SOD) and catalase. Matcha extract, a natural source of caffeine, is also the best food source of the amino acid l-theanine, which is a precursor for GABA, the neurotransmitter of relaxation. Blue Majik™ is a phenomenal COX-2 inhibiting anti-inflammatory blue pigment extract, and a tablespoon of zinc rich Styrian pumpkin seed oil or B Vitamin packed SugaVida takes the flavor to the next level!

Sling It Up

Add the coconut milk and water to a small pan and heat on the stove to about 110°F/43°C so it's just hot to the touch. Remove from stove and transfer to a heatproof container, like a Pyrex measuring cup. Add the chia seeds. Stir well, and continue stirring a couple times per minute, for about 10 minutes, or until it gelatinizes to a thick consistency.

Add the soaked chia seeds into your blender and add the rest of your ingredients.

To make a VelociTea style green chia pudding, add the additional ingredients, blend, taste, and add any additional sweetener if desired. Garnish with a swirl of Styrian pumpkin seed oil, and puffed quinoa as pictured on the left.

Panacea Panna Cotta

This recipe gives you three fantastic flavor options. The first is the mapley flavor of candy cap mushrooms. Candy caps elevate mood, help you to relax and help to relieve stress by flipping your giggle switch. With a couple of simple switch-ups, our additional flavor options are Vanilla and Lemoncello. They are sweet, they are jiggly like jello and you can enjoy them for breakfast, lunch, dinner or any time of day for a quick protein snack. These Panna Cottas are made with coconut milk (you can also use organic dairy cream) and gelatin, so they satiate your appetite, build your hair, skin and nails and will amaze all your friends!

Gather Up

2 cups (500ml) Water
3 TB Great Lakes Gelatin
4 Cups (950ml) Coconut Milk
2 TB Xylitol Powder
1 tsp Vanilla Stevia
½ tsp English Toffee Stevia

¼ tsp KAL Hazelnut Stevia
⅛ tsp Vanilla Bean Powder
½ cup (10g) Dried Candy Cap Mushrooms
2 TB Xylitol Crystals (to coat the Candy Caps)
Saigon Cinnamon (to coat the Candy Caps)

Jing It Up

2 tsp Pearl Powder

Sling It Up

In a large, covered bowl or jar, place the candy cap mushrooms in the coconut milk, and let them sit or a minimum of two hours, although it is best to soak them overnight.

In a separate glass bowl or wide mouth glass jar, place the water and a half teaspoon of vanilla stevia. Whisk in the gelatin, pouring the powder in a slow steady stream while whisking vigorously to avoid lumps from forming. Set aside for 20 minutes to fully bloom.

After the mushrooms have steeped, strain the coconut milk into your blender. Set the mushrooms aside in a separate bowl. Add the fully firmed gelatin to your blender and blend until smooth. Add xylitol powder, pearl powder, vanilla bean powder and remaining stevia to taste and blend smooth. Pour the mixture into a large saucepan and bring to simmer over low heat. Pour the warm mixture into silicone molds or tea cups and place into refrigerator to set.

To garnish: Pick out the best looking candy caps (the smaller the better) that were set aside and roll them in xylitol crystals and dust with cinnamon powder. Garnish the plated Panna Cottas with our Coconut Whipped Cream (page 74) and one of the crystalized candy caps.

For Vanilla Panna Cotta, simply omit the candy caps, toffee stevia and hazelnut stevia. Add ⅛ teaspoon of almond extract, an 1/8 tsp Vanilla Bean Powder and additional vanilla stevia to taste. Simmer and pour into molds or cups, chill to set.

For Lemoncello Panna Cotta, omit the candy caps, toffee stevia and hazelnut stevia. Add 1/2 cup of Paleo Lemon Curd (page 78) and one teaspoon of fresh, fine Lemon Zest, adjust sweetness to taste. Simmer and pour into molds or cups, chill to set.

Get the Scoop
JingLato Ice Cream

JingLato 101

There are many ways to make SuperFood Ice Cream... or as we call it, "JingLato!"

The Olympian sport of SuperFood Ice Cream pounding in a Vitamix blender began at the Erewhon Tonic Bar, a decade ago. It's pure magic to instantly whip up any kind of JingLato you want, from scratch, anytime you want it, in your very own kitchen. We use the original C-Series Vitamix blenders, they have that important "V" shape, with a narrow base. Together with a tamper stick, they provide the best blender-dynamics for instant ice cream making and for achieving the smoothest and thickest JingLato consistency possible.

We often use Coconut Ice Cubes for a frozen base. Pounding a JingLato in a typical C-Series Vitamix, you will be using one full tray of Coconut Ice Cubes and between 2-4 tablespoons of coconut milk. If you have an old-school Oster-type blender (we've got one of those too!) you will need to use different proportions. We find that an Oster-type blender works best using ¾ of a tray of Coconut Ice Cubes, and using about ¾ cup (180ml) of coconut milk. This will result in a thick smoothie consistency, which you can then put into the freezer for 1-2 hours to firm up, make into popsicles if you have pop molds, or simply enjoy it as is.

If you have a different brand of high performance blender, they will all work to different degrees. You can use a full tray of Coconut Ice Cubes with them, you will just need to add some additional coconut milk, proportions will fall between that for a Vitamix C-Series, and that of an Oster. The final result can be more of a soft serve texture, which you can always put in the freezer to firm up, if you'd like.

Making Coconut Ice Cubes is very simple. You can get creative making different types of ice cubes. We also like making them with Gynostemma Tea.

Coconut Ice Cubes

Gather Up

1½ cups (370ml, or 1 can) Coconut Milk
¼ tsp Vanilla Stevia.

Sling It Up

Stir the coconut milk and stevia together in a Pyrex-type measuring cup, dissolving any lumps in the coconut milk. If using a silicone Tovolo ice cube tray (see photo on page 98) there will be exactly enough liquid to fill it up. If you have different ice cube trays, adjust accordingly, just know that this 1½ cup (370ml) of Coconut Ice Cube measure is what we will be working with for proportions when we make our JingLato. If you do well with dairy and have access to organic raw cream, then it will also work stellar for making ice cubes.

When using Coconut Ice Cubes, once they are frozen solid, you will always want to let them sit at room temperature for about 10 minutes just before using them. This will allow them to soften just a bit. They will be much easier to pop out of their trays, and will have a little more give in the blender.

Tips on Vitamix tamper pounding method:

Depending on your physical height, and the height of your kitchen counter, you may want to stand on a sturdy single step stool, which gives you a higher angle and better leverage. As you pound your ice cream, with your free hand, press down on the blender lid, to hold the pitcher in place. Be sure to move the tamper into each corner of the blender, rotating it in clockwise and counterclockwise motions, to keep the mixture moving around the corners.

If making a double batch of JingLato, or making several JingLatos in a row, switch up your tampering arms, you'll be getting stronger forearms in the process! Start with a little bit of liquid for blending, about 2 tablespoons, and then increase from there if the consistency is too hard or too dry. You ideally want to use only as much liquid as you absolutely need to blend it, so it comes out a thick, gelato consistency.

If you have extra JingLato, you can put it into a freezer-safe non-toxic container and store in the freezer. Once it has frozen solid, let it sit at room temperature for about 45-60 minutes to soften enough to have good scoopability.

Lastly, know that JingLato isn't just dessert, it's nutritious enough to be a meal! You'll have plenty of "Jing It Up" options, including SuperFoods and Tonic Herbs as well as high quality protein powders to round out your JingLato if enjoying it as a meal. Ice cream for breakfast? Ice cream for dinner? Yes!

Most importantly, experiment with it and have fun!

PB by Jay

The power of pumpkin seed oil...This is the JingLato that started it all!

The first time Joy ever laid eyes on Jay, he was just pixels on a computer screen, demonstrating an early version of this recipe live on stage at the LongevityNow® Conference, six years ago. This is Jay's signature "Peanut Butter" JingLato with no peanuts! Peanut butter was a staple food for Jay growing up, but he ditched it because of aflatoxin issues when he first began studying health and nutrition. Years later when he discovered that the zinc and chlorophyll rich Styrian pumpkin seed oil tastes and smells just like peanut butter, he immediately recreated the favorite ice cream of his youth, only totally Jinged Up!

Instead of regular peanuts, a Jing It Up option, as pictured, is to top it with lightly toasted jungle peanuts, a clean heirloom variety of the legume. To bring out that classic peanuty flavor, place raw jungle peanuts in a pan on low heat for just a few minutes, shaking the pan, thus rolling the peanuts until lightly toasted and fragrant.

Gather Up

1 tray (400g) Coconut Ice Cubes
3 TB Lucuma Powder
3 TB Styrian Pumpkin Seed Oil
1 TB Almond Butter

1 TB Xylitol Powder
¾ tsp Toffee Stevia
¼ tsp Sea Salt
2 TB Coconut Milk

Jing It Up

1 TB Maca Powder
½ tsp Astragalus Powder
1 tsp Pearl Powder
¼ cup (38g) Roasted Jungle Peanuts

Sling It Up

Take your frozen Coconut Ice Cubes out of the freezer and let them sit on the counter for ten minutes to slightly soften. Pour the Coconut Milk into your blender. Add the softened Coconut Ice Cubes, along with the rest of your ingredients for the JingLato into your blender. Pound with your tamper, until thick and smooth. (For JingLato 101, or if you don't have a Vitamix or high performance blender, see page 100.)

Drizzle JingSlinger Chocolate Sauce (page 82) over the finished Ice Cream and gently fold, to uniformly distribute the Chocolate ribbons. Top with toasted Jungle Peanuts and Coconut Whipped Cream (page 74) and additional JingSlinger Chocolate Sauce .

Mint ice cream that's beautifying? Yep.

Chocolate ice cream that boosts energy and supports your adrenals? That's right.

Sling them up separately or together, it's always a cellular, anti-aging win-win.

Stracciatella means "little shreds," or "little ribbons " in Italian. Our "shreds?" Our JingSlinger Chocolate Sauce (page 82) , drizzled over and folded into your JingLato.

Gather Up

1 tray (400g) Coconut Ice Cubes
¼ cup (60ml) Coconut Milk
4 drops Peppermint Essential Oil
1 TB Sunflower Lecithin Powder
12 drops ChlorOxygen Chlorophyll
1 TB Xylitol Powder
¼ tsp Vanilla Stevia

Jing It Up

1 tsp Pearl Powder
2 tsp MCT Oil

Mint Stracciatella

Chocolotta Truffle JingLato

Gather Up

1 tray (400g) Coconut Ice Cubes
¼ cup (30g) Cacao Powder
1 TB Sunflower Lecithin Powder
2 TB Coconut Milk
1 TB Xylitol Powder
¼ tsp Vanilla Stevia
¼ tsp Toffee Stevia
¼ tsp Chocolate Stevia
Pinch of Sea Salt

Jing It Up

2 tsp SugaVida
1 tsp He Shou Wu
1 tsp Pearl Powder
1 TB Maca Powder
1 TB Styrian Pumpkin Seed Oil

Sling Them Up

Take your frozen Coconut Ice Cubes out of the freezer and let them sit on the counter for ten minutes to slightly soften. Pour your coconut milk into your blender. Add the softened Coconut Ice Cubes, along with the rest of your ingredients to your blender. Pound with your tamper, until smooth and thick. (For JingLato 101, or if you don't have a Vitamix or high performance blender, see page 100.)

Simply drizzle JingSlinger Chocolate Sauce (page 82) over the finished ice cream and gently fold, to uniformly distribute your beautiful chocolate ribbons.

Acai Triple Berry

This is one of our all-time favorite JingLatos. There are endless combinations of SuperFoods and Tonic Herbs that can go into this ice cream, particularly anything that plays nicely with berries. We love the anti-inflammatory effects of the acai berry and the blueberry base. E3Live Blue Majik can up the ante even further, while melding seamlessly into the flavor. Arnox Advantage increases nitric oxide and the circulatory properties of this dessert, while boosting a strawberry flavored undertone. Want it calming, with a floral undertone? Add rose water. Want to boost the anabolic effect? Add the colostrum, or add protein powder. It's easy to enjoy this JingLato on a regular basis, because it has so many options, and makes you feel so good!

Gather Up

2 packets (200g) Unsweetened Frozen Acai
¾ cup (144g) Frozen Wild Blueberries
½ cup (120 ml) Coconut Milk
½ TB Lecithin
1 TB Acai Powder
1 TB Xylitol Powder
¼ tsp Vanilla Stevia
Pinch of Sea Salt

Jing It Up

½ tsp Rose Water
½ tsp E3Live Blue Majik Powder
½ TB Arnox Advantage
½ TB Miracle Reds
2 TB Colostrum Powder
2 TB Collagen Powder, Whey
Protein, or Vanilla Vegan Protein

Primal Paleo Option

Want to take it to the next level? Add ¼ cup (100g) of grass-fed bison bone marrow. Add an additional 1-2 TB of lecithin powder to help the marrow integrate into the JingLato, which will end up with a much lighter, mousse-like consistency.

Sling It Up

Add the coconut milk to your blender. Run the acai packets under room temperature water for 3-5 seconds, then break them into 4-6 pieces and cut them open. Place the frozen acai, along with the rest of your ingredients and Jing It Up options into the blender. Pound with your tamper, until smooth and thick. (For JingLato 101, or if you don't have a Vitamix or high performance blender, see page 100.)

"I Love You Berry Much"

This strawberry ice cream is just as good as the one you had growing up, but carries more nutrition in its back pocket then most five star meals. Its fresh farm-to-table *real* strawberry flavor will take you back to the tire swing in your nana's backyard, delightfully lapping up a cone full of this homemade magic. Ice cream loves its natural match, as pictured here canoodling with our signature Chocolate Cake (page 120-121) and wrapped in our Coconut Whipped Cream (page 74).

Raise the vibration of this libation with Rose Water, which opens your heart and brightens your spirit. Did you know that Strawberries are part of the Rose family? It makes them a perfect pairing.

Gather Up

1½ cups (130g) Frozen Strawberries
⅓ tray (130g) Coconut Ice Cubes
¼ cup (60ml) Coconut Milk
1 TB Xylitol Powder
¼ tsp Vanilla Stevia
Fresh Strawberries (optional garnish)
Chocolate Covered Hemp Seeds (optional garnish)

Jing It Up

1 TB MCT Oil
1 tsp Pearl Powder
½ tsp Rose Water
½ TB Arnox Advantage
½ TB Miracle Reds
2 TB Collagen Powder, Whey Protein or Vanilla Vegan Protein

Sling It Up:

Place half of your frozen strawberries (¾ cup, 65g) in a medium-sized metal bowl and let them sit at room temperature for 10 minutes. Next, set your frozen Coconut Ice Cubes and the second half of your frozen strawberries on the counter. Let them sit for 10 minutes to slightly soften, allowing the strawberries in your metal bowl to continue softening.

Next, mash the strawberries in the metal bowl with a large fork. Pour your coconut milk into your blender and add all of your ingredients, except for the mashed strawberries in the bowl, into your blender. Pound with your tamper, until thick and smooth. (For JingLato 101, or if you don't have a Vitamix or high performance blender, see page 100.)

Spoon your JingLato out of the blender and pour into the bowl. Mix well with the mashed strawberries.

Garnish with additional fresh strawberries and chocolate covered hemp seeds.

Mojoe JingLato

This is the JingLato version of our "Love You Latte," (page 156) with a couple of different tweaks. It is a smooth, creamy coffee ice cream and we love having the extra Jing in there of the Tonic Herbs to balance the stimulating effect of the caffeine. Just like with our "Love You Latte," we have a number of Jing It Up options for extra adrenal support with the ashwagandha, he shou wu or maca powder, as well as brain and metabolism boosting effects from the MCT oil and added ghee. Add some protein and call this coffee ice cream a full-on meal that can fuel you and your "mojoe" for hours.

Gather Up

1 tray (370g) Coffee Ice Cubes
2 TB Cacao Powder
½ TB Sunflower Lecithin Powder
½ cup (120ml) Coconut Milk
¼ tsp Chocolate Stevia
¼ tsp Vanilla Stevia
¼ tsp KAL Hazelnut Stevia

Jing It Up

1 TB Ghee
1 tsp-1 TB MCT Oil
2 tsp Maca Powder
½ tsp Chaga Powder
½ tsp He Shou Wu Powder
½ tsp Ashwagandha Powder
2 TB Whey Protein, Collagen Powder
or Vanilla Vegan Protein

Sling It Up

Brew Bulletproof (or your favorite) coffee, let it cool and pour into a Tovolo ice cube trays (about 1¾ cups/430ml). Place in your freezer to freeze solid, about 3-4 hours. Once frozen solid, let your Coffee Ice Cubes sit at room temperature for 10 minutes to slightly soften. Add the coconut milk to your blender, then add your Coffee Ice Cubes and the rest of your ingredients, including your Jing It Up options. Pound with your tamper, until smooth and thick. (For JingLato 101, or if you don't have a Vitamix or high performance blender, see page 100.)

Let Them Eat Cake!

Marshmallows, Cookies, Doughnuts, Cream Puffs & CakeCuppery

High in glycine, the anabolic amino acid profile on these babies make them a beauty boosting secret weapon. In fact, the longevity properties of these may go unnoticed as they melt into your JingMaster Haute Chocolate (page 154). With no sugar to cause glycation, which lead to wrinkles, these childhood favorites are happily and healthfully back on our campfire sticks. These are an on-the-go go-to, to pop protein in a jiffy.

JingMaster Marshmallows

Gather up

⅔ cup (150 ml) water or tea for the pan

⅔ cup (150 ml) water or tea for the mixing bowl

1 tsp Pearl Powder (optional)

3 TB of Great Lakes Grass-fed Gelatin Powder

1 cup (200g) Xylitol Powder or your favorite honey

⅛ tsp Sea Salt

1 tsp Vanilla Stevia; plus ¼ tsp

⅛ tsp Almond Extract

½ tsp Vanilla Extract

½ cup (65g) Unsweetened Coconut Flakes, fine cut/macaroon cut (for coating)

Sling it up

Place ½ cup of the coconut flakes on a parchment lined cookie sheet in a 350°F/177°C degree oven for just a few minutes, until golden. Watch them carefully, they burn quickly! Remove from oven and set aside.

Line an 8x8 inch (20x20cm) square pan with two pieces of parchment paper, crossed over one another, 16x8 inches (40x20cm) each. The excess and overlapping paper will be used to lift the marshmallows out of the pan. Spray lightly with coconut oil and dust with additional xylitol powder and a generous amount of the toasted coconut flakes.

In the bowl of the stand mixer, with the whisk attachment, pour in ⅔ cup of water with ¼ tsp of vanilla stevia and then whisk in the powdered gelatin in a slow, steady stream (on low speed) until incorporated. Once fully blended, allow to spin on a low speed, to finish blooming.

Pour the other ⅔ cup of water into a medium heavy bottomed sauce pan with xylitol powder, and 1 teaspoon vanilla stevia and salt. Bring to a boil while hand whisking and use a digital heat gun (see page 33 for photo) or a candy thermometer to not exceed 240°F/116°C, this will take approximately 10-15 minutes (this is considered "soft ball stage"). Remove immediately from the heat once 240°F/116°C is reached.

Set the stand mixer speed to medium and slowly pour the hot xylitol mixture into the gelatin mixture. Once the hot xylitol mixture is in the bowl, run the mixer on high, until it expands about three times in volume.

When the marshmallow cream begins to thicken, stop the mixer. The mixture should be a soft meringue cream consistency. Now beat in the almond and vanilla extract along with the vanilla stevia until combined. Taste for sweetness and add any additional stevia if needed. Whip on high until the sweetener is fully incorporated.

Immediately pour the marshmallow cream into your parchment lined pan, smoothing with a spatula. You need to be lightening fast in this step, before it sets up! Dust the top of the marshmallows with xylitol powder and toasted coconut flakes. Let it finish setting up uncovered at room temperature for about an hour.

Lift the marshmallows from the pan by the parchment handles onto a flat surface. With a serrated knife or pizza wheel cut them into squares, or into your desired shapes with cookie cutters. Toss them in a bowl with the remaining toasted coconut and xylitol powder. Store in an air tight container for a few days for up to 2 weeks... ours never make it past a couple of days!

Jing It Up with Spring Dragon Gynostemma Tea instead of water.

Guru Goji Brilliant Brownies

These omega-3 and soluble fiber rich superfood brownies make conventional brownies blush with inadequacy. This can tune up your neurotransmitters, via "the love molecule," phenethylamine (PEA) and increase your body's level of adaptability with the goji berries. These brownies are a party pleaser, Vegan or Paleo with their dark chocolate flavor and light, moist mouth feel. Hop over to the adventurous side of entomophagy for a perfect Paleo protein profile by simply choosing the Bitty Cricket Flour option.

Gather Up

¾ cup (95g) Coconut Flour*
½ cup (65g) Cacao Powder
½ cup (100g) Xylitol Powder
¼ tsp Sea Salt
1 tsp Vanilla Extract
½ tsp Vanilla Stevia
½ tsp Chocolate Stevia
½ cup (53g) Walnuts

6 TB (90ml) Coconut Milk
½ cup (42g) Lily's Dark Chocolate Chips, melted
½ cup (110g) Coconut Oil, Super Shortening or Ghee, melted
¼ cup (28g) Goji Berries, soaked until plump and drained
2 JingSlinger "Chia Eggs" (page 136)
2 tsp MCT Oil

Jing It Up

1 tsp Pearl Powder
1 tsp He Shou Wu
1 tsp Maca Powder

* ½ cup (65g) Bitty Cricket Flour
& ¼ cup (30g) Coconut Flour
can be used to transform into
"Cricket Brownies"

Sling It Up

Pre-Heat Oven to 375°F/191°C and prepare a 12-count muffin tin with paper baking cups.

Make your chia eggs and set aside. Place the goji berries into a cup of warm water with two drops of vanilla stevia to plump and set a side. Melt the chocolate chips with the ½ cup of oil (melt them with the double boiler method, page 82). Add the vanilla extract and both stevias once the chips have melted and whisk to combine. Add the Jing It Up optional powders and whisk well.

Whisk together all the dry ingredients in a large bowl. Stir the chia eggs and coconut milk into the melted chocolate mixture while stirring briskly. Pour the wet ingredients into the dry ingredients and combine by stirring with a large spoon. Fold in the walnuts and the drained, plumped goji berries until well distributed.

Using an ice cream scoop or large spoon, fill the 12 muffin pan paper-lined cavities evenly. Smooth the tops with a wet finger. Bake at 375°F/191°C for about 30-35 minutes, checking with a toothpick in the last 10 minutes for doneness. A clean toothpick with a few moist crumbs is what you want!

These are great right out of the oven but they may be a bit crumbly, so they are best after 30 minutes or longer in the fridge to set up fully.

This is a raw, five minutes in the food processor, Vegan & Paleo friendly Praline Cookie. We love making it into layered bars and the Lemoncello Pralinedo (pictured in front of our squirrel, Gizmo). This is a body friendly and kid friendly bite of lemon sunshine. This is the perfect cookie for a little girl's teaparty or a last minute "need to bring something" notice for an unannounced get together.

Gather Up

1 cup (117g) Raw Walnuts (not soaked)
1 cup (117g) Raw Pecans (not soaked)
¼ cup (30g) Coconut Flour
2 TB SuperFood Shortening
2 TB Coconut Oil
¼ cup (50g) Xylitol Powder
3 TB Lucuma Powder

½ tsp Vanilla Bean Powder
1 tsp Lemon Juice
½ tsp Vanilla Stevia
¼ tsp Cinnamon
2 TB Unsweetened Coconut (optional garnish)

Jing It Up

1 tsp Maca Powder
¼ tsp Astragalus Powder

Sling It Up

Throw all of the ingredients into your food processor and mix until a dough forms that looks like coarse, wet sand.

Roll into a ball with your hands and then roll out to a ½ inch thick dough between two pieces of parchment paper. Chill it in the fridge until firm and then cut the desired cookie shapes with cookie cutters. Frost with the Lemon Curd Cream (page 78) and choose to make single layer or sandwich style cookies. Sprinkle with xylitol crystals, unsweetened coconut flakes, and plumped goji berries. This Praline is an awesome crumble on puddings too!

Cookie Bar Option
Press evenly into the pan or dish of choice until ½ inch thick or thicker and chill until firm. Layer with any of our "Over the Top" (page 72) fillings or creams, even a JingLato layer works great here for an ice cream bar/pie dessert. Freeze each layer as it is added one at a time.

Lemoncello
Pralinedo Cookies

BioHacking Batter 101

This is your go-to Paleo/Vegetarian Chocolate Batter recipe for everything Cake, Doughnut, CupCake, SlingShot and Whoopie Pie. With this recipe, it is the shape that makes the difference... Serious CakeCuppery is afoot! Freestyling with this batter, it doesn't matter if it is spooned into a Madeleine pan, a Doughnut mold or a 8-inch (20cm) birthday cake pan, the taste and texture aims to please. This recipe was created with flavor, function and family in mind. Mere mortals won't know that it is Grain-Free, Sugar-Free and actually good for you. You can easily double the recipe if needed. We usually make extra and freeze them to save time later. Healthy cake is officially on your plate!

Gather Up

½ cup (65g) Coconut Flour
7 TB (57g) Cacao Powder
½ cup (110ml) Coconut Oil, melted
2 TB Cacao Butter, melted
½ cup (100g) Xylitol Powder
¼ tsp Baking Soda
1 TB Water

1 tsp Lemon Juice
½ tsp Apple Cider or White Vinegar
¼ tsp Sea Salt
6 Whole Eggs, 3 separated
½ tsp Vanilla Stevia
1 tsp Chocolate Stevia

Jing It Up

1 tsp Maca Powder
1 tsp Chaga Powder
1 tsp Astragalus Powder
1 tsp Rose Water

Sling It Up

Pre-heat oven to 350°F/177°C. Lightly coconut oil the pan(s) and dust lightly with coconut flour. In cake pans, add a piece of parchment paper cut to fit the bottom of the pan.

Sift all dry ingredients into a bowl and whisk until fully incorporated. Sifting now eliminates lumps later. Place three of the separated egg whites, into your stand mixer (or a bowl to be whipped with a hand mixer later). Add all remaining wet ingredients, except for the melted cacao butter, into your blender. Blend on medium setting and while blending, pour the melted cacao butter through the lid opening in a slow, steady stream, until assimilated, then close the lid and blend on high for ten seconds. When finished, set aside.

In your stand mixer with your whisk attachment in place, whisk the three egg whites with five drops of vanilla stevia on a high speed until soft peaks are achieved. Next, pour the wet ingredients from the blender into the dry ingredients in the bowl and hand stir until there are no lumps. Gently fold the whipped egg whites into the batter using a large spoon or spatula until you have a homogenous batter with little to no egg white streaks. Immediately pour into your prepared pan(s) and place in the center rack of your oven.

Bake at 350°F/177°C until a toothpick comes out clean. It is IMPORTANT not to open the oven during the first half of the baking time, however checking with a wooden toothpick at the center of the pastry in the second half of the baking time, will tell you when it is done. The toothpick should come out mostly clean with just a couple of moist crumbs when finished baking.

Everyone's oven is different and convection ovens always bake faster. Your physical climate and elevation also affects the level of rise and length of cook time. Here are baking guidelines for this batter:

10-15 minutes for Madeleines and Whoopie Pies
30-40 minutes for 4-6 inch (10-15cm) Cakes

15-25 minutes for Cupcakes and Doughnuts
40-55 minutes for 8-10 inch (20-25cm) Cakes

Allow to cool in the fridge before icing, coating or glazing. ** See "Moist Cake Secret" on the facing page.

This Vegan Chocolate Cake Recipe does quadruple duty, just like its Paleo twin. Celebration Cakes and SuperHero Doughnuts are just a few of the CakeCuppery tricks up our JingSlinger sleeves. Creating a Vegan Cake that is sponge-cakey and moist is nothing short of pure magic, BUT when you add Sugar-Free, Gluten-Free and Soy-Free into the mix, while infusing it with SuperFoods and SuperHerbs, you are a different realm. This is feel good food for your cells. Enjoy your plant powerful Chocolate go-to for everything Cakey!

Ingredient notes: The "coconut milk" in this particular recipe was fine tuned for a lighter consistency. In testing we discovered that the Pacific Organic Coconut Milk, which is thinner then the full-fat coconut milk that we use in the majority of our other recipes produces the springy texture and lighter mouth feel we love. The benefits are in the details, which is why we use raw heirloom Arriba Nacional Cacao for our chocolate recipes. However, for a denser cake the full fat coconut milk is the ticket.

Gather Up

1¼ cup (155g) Pamela's Artisan Blend, All-Purpose Flour
1¼ cup (250g) Xylitol Powder
¾ cup (95g) Cacao Powder
½ tsp Baking Soda
1 tsp Baking Powder
3 TB Honeyville Blanched, Ultra Fine Almond Flour
1¼ cup (310ml) Pacific Unsweetened Coconut Milk

2 TB Cacao Butter, melted
½ cup (110ml) Coconut Oil, melted
2 tsp Vanilla Stevia
1 tsp Vanilla Extract
3 tsp Chocolate Stevia
2 tsp White Vinegar
2 tsp Lemon Juice
1 TB Water

Jing It Up

1 tsp Maca
1 tsp Chaga
1 tsp Astragalus
1 tsp Rose Water

Sling It Up

Preheat oven to 375°F/191°C. Lightly coconut oil the pan(s) and dust with the gluten-free flour. In cake pans, add a piece of parchment paper cut to fit the bottom of the pan.

In one large bowl, sift and combine all of the dry ingredients, except for the almond flour. In your blender, add the Pacific unsweetened coconut milk, almond flour, vanilla extract, both stevias, coconut oil, white vinegar and lemon juice and blend on a medium setting. While the wet ingredients are blending, add the melted cacao butter, then turn the blender up a notch to the next highest speed and blend for 20 seconds. Immediately pour the wet ingredients from the blender into the dry ingredients and mix with a large spoon or spatula until all the lumps are gone. Add the remaining one tablespoon of water to smooth and finish the batter if needed. Quickly pour the batter into the prepared pan(s) and place in the oven. It is important to work fast, so you don't lose the rise from the alchemical reaction that makes the cake light and springy.

Bake at 375°F/191°C in the center rack of the oven until a toothpick comes out clean. It is IMPORTANT not to open the oven during the first half of the baking time, however checking with a wooden toothpick at the center of the pastry will tell you when it is done. Everyone's oven is different and convection ovens always bake faster. Your physical climate and elevation also affects the level of rise and length of cook time. Here are baking guidelines for this batter:

10-15 minutes for Madeleines and Whoopie Pies
15-20 minutes for Cupcakes and Doughnuts
30-40 minutes for 4-6 inch (10-15cm) Cakes
40-60 minutes for 8-10 inch (20-25cm) Cakes

Allow it to cool in the fridge before icing, coating or glazing.

** JingSlinger Gluten-Free Moist Cake Secret!

While your cakes, doughnuts, etc are cooling but still warm to the touch, wrap them in parchment paper and place them in a sealed zip lock bag. This will maintain the moisture while it cools completely. Keep them stored this way until you are ready to ice them or eat them.

Thrillah Vanillah... Batter Up!

Just like its Chocolate counterpart, this Paleo/Vegetarian Vanilla Batter recipe fits all of your Grain-Free, Sugar-Free CakeCuppery baking adventures. Just the fragrant scent of vanilla bean dancing through the air in your home can be enough to boost dopamine and serotonin levels. Everything from wedding cakes to Sunday morning breakfast in bed doughnuts, get a flavorful JingSmack from the vanilloids in this SuperHero recipe which will bring out the vanilla lover in you!

Gather Up

½ cup (65g) Coconut Flour
½ cup (100g) Xylitol Powder
1 TB Water
½ cup (120ml) Coconut Oil, melted
1 tsp Vanilla Extract
2 tsp Vanilla Stevia

1 tsp Lemon Juice
½ tsp White Vinegar
⅛ tsp Vanilla Bean Powder
¼ tsp Baking Soda
⅛ tsp Sea Salt
5 Eggs, 3 separated
⅛ tsp Almond Extract

Sling It Up

Pre-heat oven to 350°F/177°C. Lightly coconut oil the pan(s) and dust lightly with coconut flour. In cake pans, add a piece of parchment paper cut to fit the bottom of the pan.

Sift all dry ingredients into a bowl and whisk until fully incorporated. Place three of the separated egg whites into your stand mixer (or a bowl to be whipped with a hand mixer later). Add all remaining wet ingredients into your blender. Pulse your blender at a low-medium speed (note: do not blend on the highest setting). Blend for about ten seconds. When finished, set aside.

In your stand mixer with your whisk attachment in place, whisk the three egg whites with five drops of vanilla stevia on a high speed until soft peaks are achieved. Next, pour the wet ingredients from the blender into the dry ingredients in the bowl and hand stir until there are no lumps. Gently fold the whipped egg whites into the batter using a large spoon or spatula until you have a homogenous batter with little to no egg white streaks. Immediately pour into your prepared pan(s) and place in the center rack of your oven.

Bake at 350°F/177°C until a toothpick comes out clean. It is IMPORTANT not to open the oven during the first half of the baking time, however checking with a wooden toothpick at the center of the pastry in the second half of the baking time, will tell you when it is done. The toothpick should come out mostly clean with just a couple of moist crumbs when finished baking.

Everyone's oven is different and convection ovens always bake faster. Your physical climate and elevation also affects the level of rise and length of cook time. Here are baking guidelines for this batter:
10-15 minutes for Madeleines and Whoopie Pies
15-25 minutes for Cupcakes and Doughnuts
30-40 minutes for 4-6 inch (10-15cm) Cakes
40-55 minutes for 8-10 inch (20-25cm) Cakes
Allow to cool in the fridge before icing, coating or glazing. ** See "Moist Cake Secret" on page (121).

Voila! Vegan Vanilla CakeCuppery for every celebration! Armed with this Gluten-Free, Sugar-Free, Soy-Free JingSlinger recipe in your "I Can't Believe It's Vegan" repertoire will have your friends saying, "Reci-Please!" Sling this better batter to avoid sugar crashes and glycation. Plus vanillic acid has also been shown in studies to alleviate inflammation via the NF-Kb and COX-2 pathways. Too much science? Just make the Cupcake!

Gather Up

1¼ cup (155g) Pamela's Artisan Blend, All-Purpose Flour
1¼ cup (250g) Xylitol Powder
½ tsp Baking Soda
1 tsp Baking Powder
⅛ tsp Vanilla Bean Powder
3 TB Honeyville Blanched, Ultra Fine Almond Flour
1¼ cup (310ml) Pacific Unsweetened Organic Coconut Milk

½ cup (110ml) Coconut Oil, melted
3 tsp Vanilla Stevia
2 tsp Vanilla Extract
2 tsp White Vinegar
2 tsp Lemon Juice
1 TB Water
½ tsp Sea Salt
⅛ tsp Almond Extract

Jing It Up

1 tsp Maca
1 tsp MCT Oil

Sling It Up

Preheat oven to 375°F/191°C. Lightly coconut oil the pan(s) and dust with the gluten-free flour. In cake pans, add a piece of parchment paper cut to fit the bottom of the pan.

In one large bowl, combine all of the dry ingredients, except for the almond flour. In your blender, add the almond flour, along with your wet ingredients: Pacific unsweetened coconut milk, vanilla extract, vanilla stevia, coconut oil, white vinegar and lemon juice and blend on a medium setting. Blend for 30 seconds. Immediately pour the wet ingredients from the blender into the dry ingredients and mix with a large spoon or spatula until all the lumps are gone. Add the remaining one tablespoon of water to smooth and finish the batter. Quickly pour the batter into the prepared pan(s) and place in the oven. It is important to work fast, so you don't lose the rise from the (al)chemical reaction that makes the cake light and springy.

Bake at 375°F/191°C in the center rack of the oven until a toothpick comes out clean. It is IMPORTANT not to open the oven during the first half of the baking time, however checking with a wooden toothpick at the center of the pastry will tell you when it is done. Everyone's oven is different and convection ovens always bake faster. Your physical climate and elevation also affects the level of rise and length of cook time. Here are baking guidelines for this batter:

10-15 minutes for Madeleines and Whoopie Pies
15-20 minutes for Cupcakes and Doughnuts
30-40 minutes for 4-6 inch (10-15cm) Cakes
40-60 minutes for 8-10 inch (20-25cm) Cakes
Allow it to cool in the fridge before icing, coating or glazing. ** See "Moist Cake Secret" on page (121).

The secret is in the shape! Now that you have a completely adaptogenic Vanilla and Chocolate BioHacked Batter recipe in your arsenal, you can make everything you see here. The marbled doughnut is simply a swirl of vanilla and chocolate batters in the doughnut pan, just before it goes in the oven. The madeleines are simply a quick tablespoon of batter and 15 minutes in the oven at 350°F/177°C for impressive tea cookies, especially when half-dipped in our JingSlinger Chocolate Sauce (page 82). The doughnuts will bake in about 15-20 minutes at the same temperature in a regular sized six-cavity doughnut pan. (Mini doughnut pan batches cook as fast as madeleines.)

The benefits here are numerous with our Gluten-Free, ketogenic ingredients. The SuperFoods that make the Chocolate Sauce and the Sugar-Free glazes elevate your butt, your belly, your brain and your beauty. Freestyle with chopped nuts, citrus zest and other SuperFood powders.

Vanilla Coconut Glaze

Gather Up

6 TB (60g) Xylitol Powder,
in a flat shallow bowl
2 tsp Collagen Powder (optional)
4 tsp Water or more
6-8 drops Vanilla Stevia
1 tsp MCT Oil
1 cup raw, unsweetened Coconut Flakes

Sling It Up

You will need two shallow bowls. In one small bowl, to create the glaze consistency, whisk in the xylitol, collagen, MCT oil and water until you get a glaze that lightly coats the back of a spoon. Add vanilla stevia to taste and whisk until fully blended. Dredge the doughnuts one at a time into the glaze and then directly into the unsweetened coconut flakes in the second flat shallow bowl.

Allow to dry and set up on a parchment lined cookie sheet or platter. They are ready to eat. You can refrigerate for 2-5 days (...but they never last that long). They do freeze beautifully if you want to hide some for later.

Jungle Peanut

Same glaze as above in the first bowl for dredging.
Place a ½ cup (75g) of raw organic jungle peanuts on a parchment lined cookie sheet in the oven while the doughnuts bake, and watch them carefully, they roast quickly and burn quickly too! Check them after a few minutes and shake the pan to roll them around a bit, roast for a few more minutes and then remove from the oven. But don't leave on the hot cookie sheet because of carryover cooking. Cool them on a piece of plain parchment on the countertop without the pan. Once cool to the touch, pulse the jungle peanuts in your coffee grinder or Vitamix until coarsely ground and place in shallow bowl for dredging with a pinch of sea salt.

Dredge the doughnuts in the glaze and them immediately into the ground jungle peanuts.
Allow to dry and set up on a parchment lined cookie sheet or platter.

Cinnamon Crusted

This is the same glaze as above but in the second bowl add 6 TB (60g) xylitol crystals and 4-6 generous teaspoons of cinnamon powder to taste for the dredging. We love Saigon Cinnamon, it's heavenly. All three of these doughnuts taste even better after being in the fridge overnight.

JingSlingers' SuperHero Doughnuts

SlingShots

These cute, Cosmic Doughnut Holes cause quite a ruckus whenever we bring them to a celebration. Sugar-Free, Gluten-Free, even Grain-Free or Vegan, it's your choice! Their SuperFood ingredients, especially their fat burning chocolate coat, enchants Paleo, Vegan and Omnivore Foodies alike. You get to Sling them how you love them. They are # 1 on our "Most Wanted" list! To create these bouncy balls in your very own kitchen, you will need either an electric cake pop maker or the old-school, two-piece cake ball pans for your oven (they also have silicone cake ball pans, see photo on page 33). We use all three methods, but in a time crunch, the electric cake pop maker reigns supreme, we're talking a dozen balls done every 5 minutes, until your batter runs out. Using either a piping bag, or a non-BPA batter bottle makes filling the pan cavities fast and clean.

Gather Up

JingSlinger Paleo or Vegan Chocolate Batter
Recipe of your Choice (pages 120-121)
JingSlinger Chocolate Sauce Recipe (page 82)
3 cups (240g) Puffed Quinoa
Peppermint Essential Oil (optional)

Jing It Up

1 TB Rose Water
2 tsp Astragalus Powder
2 tsp Pearl Powder
2 tsp Restore the Jing

Sling It Up

Mix the JingSlinger Chocolate Batter Recipe (this is where you mix in the Jing It Up options into the batter) and fill the batter bottle or piping bag, or you can just spoon it. Lightly coconut oil the cavities of your cake pop maker or the ball pans. Plug in and pre-heat your electric pop maker, until it indicates it is ready to go. For pan baking, pre-heat your oven to 350°F/177°C. Fill the cavities to the very top, being careful not to overfill. This will ensure a good rise from the batter, creating the perfect orb.

Once the cake balls are ready from the pop maker, set them aside to cool. To test the doneness of the cake balls in the oven, check with a toothpick through the hole in the center of the pan until it comes out clean. Begin checking after the first ten minutes. They usually cook in about 15-20 minutes in the oven. In the electric cake ball maker, they cook in five minutes or less. The indicator light will tell you.

Cool the cake balls in the refrigerator for about 30 minutes, now you are ready to dunk.

Prepare the JingSlinger Chocolate Sauce recipe. If you choose to make our signature "AahhMazeMints" (they taste like Thin Mint Girl Scout Cookies) simply add 3-4 single drops of the peppermint essential oil into the chocolate sauce and stir. Add this mint to taste, a little bit goes a long way!

Fill a wide, shallow bowl with puffed quinoa and a second bowl with the hot chocolate sauce. Dunk two naked cake balls at a time into the chocolate sauce. Roll, coat and drain using a large slotted or vented metal spoon or spider. Immediately drop into the bowl of puffed quinoa, and completely cover them using your fingers. Set them aside on a parchment lined baking sheet to cool and firm up in the refrigerator.

Additional flavors are up to your imagination. Check out our doughnut glazes and coatings on the preceding two pages for inspiration. Have a ball with your new balls!

"The Cacao Jumped

Over the Moon" CakePhoria

Flourless, Grain-Free, Sugar-Free, Paleo Chocolate Cake Bliss... this is a magnesium, anandamide and protein packed behemoth, it is a celebration on a plate! Dress this with Coconut Whipped Cream, fresh berries and a drizzle of our melted JingSlinger Chocolate Sauce for a 5 star restaurant experience without a sugar crash. The stress reducing magnesium and mood elevating anandamide are nutritional ninjas that will help centered and somewhat euphoric... hence "CakePhoria!"

Gather Up

16 oz (454g) Lily's Sugar-Free Dark Chocolate Baking Chips
(or Lily's Bars, chopped)
10 Large Eggs, separate the yolks from the white
(no yolks at all in the whites!)
¾ - 1 cup of Xylitol Powder (or more to taste)
8 TB (112g) Unsalted Butter
1 tsp Vanilla Extract
½ tsp Vanilla Stevia
1 tsp Chocolate Stevia
⅛ tsp Cream of Tarter
Fresh Raspberries (optional garnish)

Jing It Up

2 tsp Restore the Jing
1 tsp Pearl Powder
1 tsp Maca Powder
1 tsp Chaga Powder

Sling It Up

Preheat the oven to 350°F/177°C.

Butter an 8, 9, or 10-inch (20, 23, or 25cm) spring form pan or several 3 or 4-inch (8 or 10cm) cake pans for individual servings and place an unbleached circle of parchment in the bottom. (We always wrap the outside bottom of the spring form pan with tin foil so no water seeps into the cake pan while baking.) Add 2 inches of hot water into a larger oven safe pan so your cake bakes in a water bath.

Put the chocolate chips/ chopped bars and butter into the top of a double boiler (or in a heatproof metal bowl) and heat over (but not touching) about 1 inch of simmering water until melted.

Meanwhile, whisk the egg yolks with the xylitol powder in a mixing bowl until light yellow in color. Whisk a little of the chocolate mixture into the egg yolk mixture, once the chocolate has fully melted, to temper the eggs - this will keep the eggs from scrambling from the heat of the chocolate - then whisk in the rest of the chocolate mixture, stirring in the herbs, vanilla extract and vanilla stevia & chocolate stevia. Set aside.

Beat the egg whites and cream of tarter in a mixing bowl until stiff peaks form (a stand mixer works best, but an electric hand mixer works too). Now fold the chocolate mixture into the egg white mixture a quarter at a time, with a large spoon or spatula until it becomes a well-incorporated chocolate batter. Pour into the prepared pan and bake for about 35-45 minutes, until a toothpick inserted into the cake comes out mostly clean with some moist crumbs. Let it cool for about 30 minutes at room temperature and then chill in fridge for an additional 20-30 minutes to set. Then you can remove the sides of pan. For the small pans, run a knife or thin bladed spatula around the inside edge to release the cake.

Serve cake at room temperature with berries and topped with Coconut Whipped Cream (page 74).

Mama's Got New Choux!

Joy loves this recipe for Epic Éclairs, it is a go-to for so many of our Pâte À Choux delights! Even though she was a Police Officer for 20 years, doughnuts were not her thing, BUT an Éclair was, and still is her favorite. The benefits of these renovated Éclairs are hormone balancing thanks to the Maca Powder and fat burning thanks to the SuperFood Coconut Cream filling choices and JingSmacked Chocolate Glaze. Churros, Profiteroles, Gougeres, Beignets, and yes… even Paleo Gnocci! They are all made from this base recipe. These babies also make awesome Paleo hamburger/sandwich buns by simply leaving out the stevia and piping or spooning the dough into a larger, round shape. You can freestyle a personal pizza crust or savory tart crust too.

Gather Up

1 cup (125g) Otto's Cassava Flour
1 cup (250ml) Water
1 cup (250ml) Eggs (or 4 large Eggs)
1 stick (8 TB or 113g) Unsalted Butter
½ tsp Vanilla Stevia*
⅛ tsp Sea Salt

Egg Wash

1 Egg
1 TB Water
3 drops Vanilla Stevia*

(*If it's for a savory recipe, you can eliminate the Stevia)

Jing It Up

½ tsp Maca Powder
1 tsp SugaVida

Sling It Up

Preheat oven to 425°F/218°C. Line a large cookie sheet with parchment paper. Whisk or sift the flours together along with the salt, SugaVida and maca, in a large bowl until it is well combined, and set it aside.

In a saucepan, on low to medium heat, melt the butter or shortening into the water until you see the first few bubbles, but do not allow it to boil. Remove from the heat and pour the flour mixture into the hot, wet mixture, stirring gingerly until it forms a big, soft dough. Immediately, place the dough into your stand mixer with the paddle attachment in place, spin on the lowest speed and allow the dough to cool down by mixing it for about a minute and a half. If mixing by hand, remove the pan from the heat and beat in one egg at a time and add each additional egg, one at a time, mixing the batter until each egg is fully incorporated into the dough.

You should now have a thick, sticky dough that is stiff enough to pipe. Either scoop with a spoon or pipe with a pastry bag (with 1M tip) or simply cut the corner point off of a zip lock bag after you have loaded it with the dough. Pipe onto the parchment paper in a rounded 2-inch mound for Cream Puffs or a 5-6 inch line for Éclairs. Pipe them about two inches apart to allow for expansion. (Joy also loves to make heart shaped cream puffs, about the size of a small dinner roll.)

Brush with the egg wash, smoothing down any peaks with your fingers and set them in the middle of the oven on the center rack to bake for about 10 minutes at 425°F/218°C.

Do not open the door of the oven while the high heat does its work! Watch through the oven's window and lower the temperature to 375°F/191°C after 10 minutes. Bake for another 15-20 minutes for smaller puffs and 20-25 minutes for the larger Éclairs until they puff up tall, golden and firm to the touch. If you are not sure if they are done, pull one out carefully and set it out to cool. If it collapses, they are not ready and your oven temperature may not have been hot enough. Bake for an additional 5-10 minutes, watching them like a hawk so they don't over bake. You have now mastered Pâte À Choux! Cool and slice in half. Dip the top half in JingSlinger Chocolate Sauce (page 82) and then fill with the Coconut Whipped Cream Filling (page 74) just before serving. Now watch them disappear!

The unglazed, unfilled pastry shells will keep in an airtight container for 3-4 days in the refrigerator. In the freezer, they will keep for 2-3 weeks. Do not defrost, simply reheat the already baked shells in the oven. Freezing the piped dough on the parchment paper in a sealed container and then baking them without thawing them works best for an upcoming dinner or event if you need to save time. Freestyle with the fillings! Pictured are coconut cream with cacao powder and Wildberry Cream (page 74).

Vanilla Bean

Shortbread Pie Crust

Gather Up

1½ cups (160g) fine milled Almond Flour
2 TB Arrowroot Flour
3 TB Xylitol Powder
2 TB Coconut Milk
3 TB Ghee or SuperFood Shortening

½ tsp Vanilla Extract
½ tsp Vanilla Stevia
1 tsp MCT Oil
½ tsp Psyllium Husk Powder
⅛ tsp Sea Salt

Jing It Up

2 tsp Pearl Powder
1 tsp Maca Powder
⅛ tsp Vanilla Bean Powder

Sling Them Up

Preheat oven to 350°F/177°C. You will need a 9-inch (23cm) pie or tart pan.

Stir all the dry ingredients in a medium bowl until well combined. Add the wet ingredients and stir with a spoon until a pliable, soft dough forms. Shape the dough by hand into a thick disk. Wrap in parchment paper tightly, place in a plastic bag and chill in the refrigerator until slightly firm, about 10 minutes. Place the chilled dough between two pieces of parchment on a flat surface and begin to flatten with the palm of your hand. Finish shaping the dough with a rolling pin until it is uniformly about ⅛ inch thick. Rolling pin rings (see photo on page 33) will help you get the right thickness. Remove the top parchment and place the pie pan upside down onto the dough. Slide a thin piece of cardboard (or a cake round) underneath the parchment to keep the crust from cracking, as you quickly flip it over for the crust to settle into the pan. Cut off any excess dough and redistribute with your fingers. Pat and smooth the crust to fit the shape of the pan. Chill in the fridge for about 10-15 minutes. Place in the oven on the center rack to bake, about 30-35 minutes, or until firm to the touch.

Fill with your favorite filling and serve. We love to fill our sweet crusts with our Coconut Crème Brûlée (page 92), Lemon Curd (page 78) and top with Coconut Whipped Cream (page 74) and Jing Jam (page 80).

*Chef Note – You can simply form the dough into your pan of choice with your hands until evenly distributed. This does not require you to chill it in the refrigerator before forming the crust or to use a rolling pin.

Cacao Shortbread Pie Crust

Gather Up

1½ cups (160g) fine milled Almond Flour
5 TB (40g) Cacao Powder
3 TB Xylitol Powder
¼ cup Ghee or SuperFood Shortening
2 TB Coconut Milk, chilled
1 TB Water

1 tsp MCT Oil
1 tsp Psyllium Husk Powder
½ tsp Chocolate Stevia
½ tsp Vanilla Stevia
⅛ tsp Sea Salt
¼ tsp Vanilla Extract

Jing It Up

1 tsp Maca Powder
1 tsp Pearl Powder
½ tsp He Shou Wu Powder
3 TB SugaVida (instead of Xylitol)

*Sling It Up Instructions are on the facing page.

JingSlinger Savory Pie Crust

Gather Up

1½ cups (160g) fine milled Almond Flour
2 TB Otto's Cassava Flour
3 TB Ghee or SuperFood Shortening
1 tsp Psyllium Husk Powder

3 TB Coconut Milk
½ tsp Black Pepper
½ tsp Black Truffle Salt or Sea Salt
½ tsp Garlic Granules
1 TB Water

Jing It Up

1 tsp MCT Oil
2 tsp Pearl Powder
1 tsp Maca Powder

All three of these Sugar-Free, Grain-Free, Paleo & Vegan Pie Crusts Sling Up as a 1-bowl, 1-spoon recipe. We use Honeyville fine milled Almond Flour because it is consistent in flavor and texture, making it the perfect flour for pastries and baking.

The Sling It Up instructions are the same for all three of these crusts.

Beyond the Plate...

How to Make Ice Cream Anytime 101...

Being able to Sling Ice Cream anywhere is magical with or without a blender!

This Ice Cream Ball brings *Playing With Your Food* to a new level of fun because it can be at a soccer practice, a tailgate party, camping or in your back yard and in just 30 to 45 minutes a healthy JingLato appears! It works with full-fat coconut milk or grass-fed cream in any flavor you wish. Jason and Whitney played catch until our coconut milk-based Vanilla Bean Salted Caramel JingLato materialized.

You can also make a single serving of ice cream with a ball jar, a bag of ice and a little rock salt.

The Ball recipe is 4 cups of full fat coconut milk, 1 tsp vanilla stevia, ½ tsp vanilla bean powder, ¼ tsp vanilla extract, 2 Tablespoons of Xylitol and pieces of our Salted Caramel Crunchies, (Nuts or Lily's Sugar-Free Chocolate Chips would be great here too.) Load the ball with ice cubes and a bit of rock salt. In the sealed inner cavity pour in the ingredients and the motion of the ball churns the contents into ice cream in minutes.

"Done in 60 Seconds" Blueberry Semifreddo

Trick # 1 - Stir one cup of frozen blueberries, right out of the freezer, into one cup of coconut yogurt, or any Greek Style Yogurt. The temperature of the berries immediately thickens and freezes the yogurt into a scoopable instant Blueberry Semifreddo. Your kids will think you are magic.

Trick # 2 - Instant Ice Cream - Refrigerate two cans of coconut milk overnight. Without shaking the cans, carefully open them, and scoop out just the coconut cream, collected from the top of the can. Save the remaining coconut water for future recipes.

With the whisk attached, place coconut cream into the bowl of your stand mixer or into a metal bowl with a hand mixer. Beat on high speed and sift in 3 tablespoons of cacao powder and any additional flavors, extracts or essential oils (like mint) you wish to infuse (a little bit at a time). After about 3 minutes, stop the mixer, scrape down the sides and add additional sweetener to balance the flavors you have chosen. Add a few drops of vanilla stevia or chocolate stevia at a time, to taste and give it one more spin. It is now ready to eat as soft serve, or place it in the freezer for about 20-30 minutes to firm up like gelato.

JingSlinger Vegan Egg Replacement 101

When you Google "Vegan Egg Replacement" and everything from applesauce to flax eggs pop up, what's a chef to do? After testing hundreds of recipes designed for our discerning Vegan clients, the popular "1 tablespoon chia seed to 3 tablespoons of water" falls short for both taste and chemistry... it works okay, but it is not stellar. Our science geekitude is showing again, so hang with us this is a good thing!

First objective, how does it behave in the texture of your muffin/cake? Second objective, how does it behave in your body? We prefer chia to flax first because it packs more protein like an egg would and chia is not über estrogenic, so it doesn't jack with your hormones. Chia seeds do not go rancid with the same quickness that flax tends to, and trust us, you don't want rancid oils in your blood stream! Our JingSlinger Chia Egg is based on the culinary chemistry one large chicken egg brings to the table in baking for both flavor and texture.

Gather Up

1 TB freshly ground Chia Seed, measured after the grinding...
über important detail (there is the protein profile we want)
4 TB warm Water
1 tsp Coconut Oil (for the healthy fat component)

Beyond the Plate...

Sling It Up

Pour the 4 tablespoons of water and the 1 teaspoon of oil into a small bowl. Grind the chia seeds in your coffee or spice grinder, or powderize old-school style with a mortar and pestle, until you get a fine powder. Measure the 1 level tablespoon of the now ground chia into the water, a little at a time while whisking briskly to avoid clumps. Let it do its gel thing either on the counter top or in the fridge. When you measure it into a recipe, it will be 4 level tablespoons of the now gelled chia egg mixture for each egg called for in the recipe.

So one large egg equals = 4 tablespoons of a JingSlinger Chia Egg.
One cup of eggs equals = 4 JingSlinger Chia Eggs.

Note that a chia egg does not provide much or any rise or lift but it does allow the batter to come together and the protein aspect keeps it together. This egg does not whip into meringue or work in Pâte À Choux recipes. Chia eggs do impart a slight nutty flavor not so noticeable in chocolate or spice cake type recipes but in vanilla you may detect it. For lift and rise and a fluffy or more tender cake, muffin or cupcake you gotta deploy the special alchemical forces of lemon juice, apple cider or white vinegar with baking soda and or aluminum-free, non-GMO baking powder.

*It should be noted that we had the pleasure of testing the first release of the much-anticipated "Follow Your Heart" brand "Vegan Egg." It scrambles awesome, making fluffy eggs, especially when you mix it with super cold water directly from the fridge and blast it on the high speed setting of your blender to mix the Vegan Egg powder and water together to create your egg. Add black truffle salt and chives and they are yum! It makes a great omelet and even works well in making matzo balls for our Chickenless Matzo Ball soup.

We did not find that it works for the rise in baked goods that an egg provides. However, the result was the same as the JingSlinger Chia Egg when tested head-to-head in the same recipe, deploying all three choices evenly. We do love that the base of this product is algae and an algae protein. The downside is that they included carrageenan into the mix and that, unfortunately is an additive we avoid, especially if this is something you will consume regularly.

Liquid Assets

Got Jing?

Liquid Assets

Blender Bending

Living Waters Margarita

Inspired by one of the original drinks from the Erewhon Tonic Bar, this is a live probiotic, hydrating and alkalizing drink that is our go-to for recovery whenever we are arrive back home after flying and traveling. It is also a great thing to reach for after a hard workout!

This recipe will make enough for 2-4 people, however, even if you are enjoying it by yourself, know that it will keep well in the refrigerator for at least 3-4 days. If you are purchasing coconut water kefir, it will usually be packaged in a 16 ounce bottle, so to save time and money, we based the proportions around one full bottle. Because this is a live fermentation, be sure to seal it in a jar or container with an airtight lid. Remember... Your margarita is alive! Pressure can build up in the bottle, so open it carefully over your sink. Always open coconut water kefir bottles the same way! (see page 158 for more info)

Gather up

3 cups (420g) Ice
1½ cups (370ml) Water
2 cups (250ml) Coconut Water Kefir
½ cup (120ml) Lemon Juice
1 TB Lemon Rind
2 tsp Fresh Grated Ginger or 1 TB Ginger Juice
½ cup (120ml) Coconut Milk
1 TB Styrian Pumpkin Seed Oil
¼ tsp Vanilla Stevia (or more to taste)
¼ tsp Sea Salt

Jing It Up!

½ tsp ChlorOxygen
¼ cup (60ml) Aloe Juice/ fresh Aloe Gel
¼ cup (30g) Vanilla Whey Protein or Vegan Protein
¼ cup (30g) Collagen Powder
2 tsp Pearl Powder

Sling it up

Toss all ingredients into a high performance blender and blend well. Know that this drink will expand, so do not overfill your blender. Better to blend in batches, in equal halves.

Helixir & Shelixir

This shot can have a powerful effect on your date night and your immunity!
You can choose to Jing It Up or Shen It Out and still have ALL the energy
you need for extracurricular activities. This can be a hot or cold shot, you
Sling it how you wish!

Gather Up

4 cups (1000ml) Apple Cider
2 tsp Unsweetened Mulling Spice or Cinnamon
½ tsp Pearl Powder (optional)
1 tsp Deer Antler (or Dragon Herbs Cistanche Extract for a Vegan Shot)
1 tsp Ionic Mineralife Magnesium
2 drops Vanilla Stevia (or more to taste)
1 tsp Maca Powder

Sling It Up

Whirl in the blender
or shake in a martini
shaker, serve hot
or over crushed ice...

Shaken not stirred...

Garnish with an apple
slice, blackberries
or just naked.

Along with our Living Waters Margarita and our Strawberry Lemontini, this drink is part of our JingSlinger Hydration Trifecta and utilizes the juiciness of fresh cucumbers. The phrase of being "cool as a cucumber" contains a lot of truth, not only can cucumbers help to lower inflammation, they also contain many nutrients including B Vitamins, which help us to handle stress. Pair it with the sweet tropical flavor of frozen (or fresh) pineapple, another notorious anti-inflammatory food, high in the proteolytic enzyme bromelain, and then Jing It Up with aloe vera, one of the best cooling, soothing, moistening foods in Ayurveda, and you have a sure fire recipe for cellular hydration and relaxation.

Cucumber-Pineapple

Gather Up

2 cups (500ml) fresh Cucumber Juice
8oz (225g) Frozen Pineapple
¼ cup (60ml) Coconut Milk
¼ tsp Vanilla Stevia
¼ tsp Sea Salt

Jing It Up!

¼ cup (60ml) Aloe Juice or Aloe Gel

Sling It Up

Juice two medium cucumbers, or conveniently buy raw cucumber juice at a local juice bar. Add your pineapple to the blender, add the rest of your ingredients and blend well for about 20-30 seconds. Taste it and add more vanilla stevia if you would like it sweeter. Enjoy it in one sitting, or share with a friend. We usually made a whole blender of this, and it's magically gone within minutes!

146

Strawberry Basil Lemontini

Sweet, sour, salty, savory… this drink hits all the right buttons and pulls all the right switches on your palate. Equally fitting for casual get togethers, or for formal affairs, our Strawberry Basil Lemontini always results in glasses being drained in record time. Enjoy the flavor, feel the hydration, while benefiting from the detoxifying properties of the lemon and strawberry, and the natural antibacterial and anti-inflammatory effects of the basil. Whatever flavor or factoid you like best about it, we know you'll be scrambling for seconds!

Gather Up

10 oz (284g) Frozen Strawberries
2 TB Lemon Juice
1 TB Lemon Rind
5 medium-large fresh Basil Leaves
2 TB Coconut Milk
2 cups (500ml) Water
1 TB Xylitol
¼ tsp Vanilla Stevia
¼ tsp Sea Salt

Jing It Up

2 TB Aloe Vera Juice or Fresh Gel
½ TB Arnox Advantage

Sling It Up

Place frozen strawberries into your blender, along with the rest of your ingredients, adding the water last. Blend well. If you want a thinner consistency, add ¼ cup (60ml) of water at a time, until desired consistency is reached.

Into the Blue

Jump start your morning by Slinging this raw dark chocolate smoothie for a magnesium bump, to rev up your brain and burn some fat. Spoon in our favorite ancient wisdom longevity secrets with he shou wu, maca and ashwagandha. Acai's resveratrol, anthocyanidins, and polyphenols kick up the antioxidants while the brilliant blue phycocyanins from the E3Live Blue Majik help to extinquish inflammation. This is where beauty meets anti-aging and total yum! Vegans can add hemp seeds and Paleo folks can Sling it with collagen protein and colostrum powder.

Gather Up

½ cup (120ml) Water
2 cups (500ml) Coconut Milk
1 cup (187g) Wild Blueberries, frozen
¼ cup (30g) Cacao Powder
1 TB Acai Powder
1 TB Maca Powder
1 tsp Pearl Powder
½ tsp E3Live Blue Majik
¼ tsp Vanilla Stevia
¼ tsp Chocolate Stevia
1 TB Xylitol Powder

Jing It Up

2 TB Collagen Powder
2 TB Colostrum Powder
1 tsp He Shou Wu Powder
1 tsp Ashwagandha Powder
½ TB Arnox Advantage

Sling It Up

Add all of your ingredients except for the Blue Majik, into your blender and blast it on high! Blend well, until smooth. Add Blue Majik on top when serving and swirl with a spoon. Garnish with a few extra blueberries.

BLUcidity

The SuperFoods in the BLUcidity Shot support a brilliant brain, beaming beauty, while banishing body aches with powerful primordial foods! This is the brain shot that we made live on Dave Asprey's Bulletproof Podcast # 145.

The PEA of the E3Live Brain On tickles your tongue and feeds your brain, boosting many important neurotransmitters. The collagen and pearl bolster your skin's regeneration and luminosity, while the natural COX-2 inhibiting properties of the Blue Majik phycocyanin (blue pigment) concentrate banishing body aches. Lion's mane mushroom is an immune powerhouse, and protects your nervous system in many unique ways. Enjoy BLUcidity as a daily tonic shot, or anytime you need extra brain power or creative thinking.

Gather up

1 cup (240ml) Coconut Milk
1 tsp - 1 TB MCT Oil
½ tsp E3Live Blue Majik Powder
½ tsp E3Live Brain On Powder
1 tsp Host Defense Lion's Mane (open up 4 capsules)
⅛ - ¼ tsp Vanilla Stevia (to taste)
⅛ - ¼ tsp Chocolate Stevia (to taste)

Jing It Up

1 TB Colostrum Powder
1 TB Collagen Powder
½ tsp Pearl Powder
¼ tsp Deer Antler Extract
½ tsp Vanilla Bean Powder

Sling it up

Pour the coconut milk and MCT oil into a small bowl. Mix in the dry powders with a whisk or spoon until fully integrated into the coconut milk and MCT oil. It will be a beautiful shade of blue! Add your vanilla and chocolate stevia to taste.

"Miso Yin" Soup

Yin is the energetic principle of rest, repair, recovery and rejuvenation. This SuperFood Blender Soup is perfect for winding down at the end of your day and preparing you for the most Yin thing you do... sleep. Kelp is an amazing Yin food. We pair kelp granules from the company Maine Coast in this recipe with several other nutritives and tonic herbs that enhance relaxation to help you fall asleep, and provide the nourishment for a deep, rejuvenative sleep.

The organic, non-GMO, 2-3 year fermented "Hacho Miso" from Eden Foods is the only appearance of soybean in any form in this book. This miso is a nutritious, probiotic, grounding food, which is fermented in a 650-year old traditional manner using bamboo barrels.

SugaVida takes the flavor of this soup through the roof, while its array of B Vitamins provide the building blocks for a deep night's sleep. Our favorite Ionic Magnesium, from Mineralife, is an amazing Jing It Up option. Magnesium before bed helps you sleep like a rock, and will help with testosterone production in the morning, especially for men. Add collagen protein, Sea Tangle Kelp Noodles, Miracle Noodles, or our Sweet Potato Naan (pictured left, see page 192) if you wish to make this soup even more hearty.

Gather Up

1½ cup (370ml) Water
½ cup (120ml) Coconut Milk
2 TB Kelp Granules
1 TB Hacho Miso
1 TB Black Sesame Seed
1 tsp Yellow Curry Powder

½ tsp Fajita Powder
2 tsp Lemon Juice
1 TB Ghee/ SuperFood Shortening
1 tsp Pearl Powder
2 tsp SugaVida
Sea Tangle Kelp Noodles (optional)

Jing It Up

½ tsp Restore the Shen
½ tsp Mucuna
1 TB Collagen
1 tsp Mineralife Ionic Magnesium

Sling It Up

Place kelp noodles in hot water or hot gynostemma tea to hydrate and soften. Drain before adding into the soup.

Add the water and coconut milk to a small pan on the stove and bring it to a simmer. Add all of your additional ingredients (except for the optional noodles) into your blender. Add your hot liquid to your blender, put your blender lid on and cover the lid with a towel. Hold the lid down, as you turn the blender on the lowest setting, before cranking up to high. Blend on high for 45-60 seconds.

Jinged Up Option Combos

For additional Macronutrients, add Ghee or SuperFood Shortening and/or Collagen Powder

For Jing Boosting and Adrenal Fortification, add Maca, Restore the Jing and/or He Shou Wu Powder

For Calming and Serenity Enhancement, add Reishi Mushroom, Awaken the Shen and/or Pear Powder

For Immune Boosting Effects, add Reishi Mushroom, Chaga Mushroom and/or Vanilla Bean Powder.

For Micronutrients, Mapley Flavor and Mood Enhancement, add SugaVida and/or Candy Cap Mushroom

For Ayurvedic Nervous System Nourishment, add Ashwagandha Root and/or Mucuna Powder

JingSlinger Haute Chocolate

JingSlinger Haute Chocolate... there is no single way to Sling it! Here we have our base recipe for our SuperFood Haute Chocolate, with several ways of Slinging It with bonus SuperFoods and Tonic Herbs. One of the great things about Haute Chocolate is that you can incorporate earthy, bitter tasting herbs more easily then most other drinks because they lean into the flavor of the chocolate, instead of sticking out like a sore thumb.

Whenever using hot liquid in your blender, your blender will build up pressure quickly. Make sure you have a towel over your lid and begin blending on your lowest setting, before bringing it to a pulverizing high speed. Otherwise you might be painting your ceiling with your elixir!

Gather Up

1 cup (250ml) Coconut Milk
1 cup (250ml) Water
3 TB Cacao Powder
1 tsp Cacao Butter
¼ tsp Cinnamon Powder
¼ tsp Vanilla Stevia
¼ tsp Chocolate Stevia
¼ tsp Toffee Stevia
1 tsp Xylitol

Jing It Up!

1 TB Ghee/ SuperFood Shortening
2 TB Collagen Powder
1 tsp Maca Powder
½ tsp He Shou Wu
½ tsp Reishi Mushroom Powder
½ tsp Chaga Mushroom Powder
½ tsp Restore the Jing
½ tsp Awaken the Shen

½ tsp Pearl Powder
½ tsp Vanilla Powder
2 tsp SugaVida
½ tsp Mucuna Powder
½ tsp Ashwagandha Powder
¼ - ½ tsp Candy Cap Mushrooms

Sling It Up!

In a small pot, heat the Coconut Milk and Water to a soft boil.

Add your base ingredients into your blender, as well as any of the Jinged It Up options. Pour your hot liquids into the blender, put the lid on, hold the lid down tightly making sure the vents can still breathe, and blend on the lowest setting, gradually ramping it up to a high blend and blending well, for 30 seconds.

I Love You Latte

Now the Coffee you Love, can Love you back! We use Bulletproof Coffee as the base for this Latte. It insures an upgraded coffee experience from their uber clean beans. Coffee is an excellent potentiator for deep delivery of important macronutrients and tonic herbs. We love balancing the natural caffeine bump in our latte with herbs that support your adrenals, and healthy fats that support your hormones and brain function.

Our preferred method for brewing coffee is the French Press method. From start to finish, it takes less then five minutes!

Gather Up

2 cups (500ml) brewed Coffee
2 TB Cacao Powder
1 TB Sunflower Lecithin Powder
2 TB Collagen Powder (Paleo Option)
2 TB Ghee or SuperFood Shortening
½ tsp KAL brand Hazelnut Stevia
½ tsp Vanilla Creme Stevia
½ tsp Chocolate Stevia
¼ cup (60ml) Coconut Milk

Jing It Up

1 tsp Restore the Jing
1 tsp Pearl Powder
1 TB Maca Powder
1 tsp - 1 TB MCT Oil

Sling It Up

Place all ingredients in your blender. Cover with a towel and hold the lid down tightly, allowing the vents to still breathe and blend starting on the lowest setting, gradually ramping it up to a high speed and blending well, for 30 seconds.

Sleeping BeauTea

Want to biohack your sleep? Combining nutraceuticals, minerals and Chinese & Ayurvedic Tonic Herbs, this is our ultimate herbal sleep tea!

Awaken the Shen is calming and heart opening, while pearl powder is soothing and grounding. L-theanine is a GABA precursor, your neurotransmitter for relaxation. Ashwagandha can help to regulate sleep patterns, and also influences GABA pathways. Bupleurum & Dragon Bone is a Vegan option to replace the pearl powder, it is a classic Chinese herbal formula that helps to relieve stress by relieving liver stagnation and is also used to help curb addiction. 5-HTP is a precursor to melatonin, the neurotransmitter of the sleep cycle. Magnesium, the mineral of calmness, adds another layer of deep sleep and rejuvenation, while SugaVida provides crucial micronutrients.

Want to take it one step further? Use the adaptogenic herb Gynostemma for your tea base in Spring Dragon Tea. Let the stress of the day roll off your back, and may deep, delta, stage 4 sleep be your new best friend.

Gather Up

1 cup (250ml) Water
½ cup (120ml) Coconut Milk
½ tsp Awaken the Shen
½ tsp Pearl Powder
½ tsp Ashwagandha
1 capsule (200mg) L-Theanine

1 TB Lucuma Powder
½ TB Ghee or SuperFood Shortening
¼ tsp Cinnamon Powder
¼ tsp Vanilla Stevia
¼ tsp Toffee Stevia

Jing It Up

Spring Dragon Tea
1 capsule (100mg) 5-HTP
½ tsp Bupleurum & Dragon Bone
1 tsp Mineralife Magnesium
2 tsp SugaVida

Sling It Up

In a small pan, combine the water and coconut milk and bring to a light boil. If you are using Spring Dragon Tea for your base, then bring just the water to a boil and turn the heat off and allow the teabag steep for 5 minutes. Remove the teabag, add the coconut milk, and continue warming to a simmer.

Place all ingredients in your blender, adding your hot liquid last. Cover the lid with a towel, making sure the lid is vented. Hold the lid down tightly. Blend on the lowest setting, gradually ramping it up to a high speed and blending well, for 30 seconds

Beyond the Plate...

Coco Jack

Ever wonder if there was a fast, simply way to open a fresh Thai coconut without lopping off a limb?

This cool tool not only saves your digits, it saves a lot of time and effort, especially if you frequent Asian markets and buy your coconuts by the case.

The "Coco Jack" is as easy to use as it looks. While the opening of the coconut is smart, the little scoop for scraping out the coconut meat in one big piece, in about 5 seconds flat, will impress the heck out of anyone who has ever opened a raw coconut any other way.

Coconut Water Kefir

Kefir is alive! Always open bottles of coconut water kefir SLOWLY. Release the cap just a little bit to see how much pressure is in there. Sometimes you can open them all the way right away, but sometimes you have to keep letting the pressure off bit-by-bit by opening the cap just a little, then quickly closing it. You can tell by whether there are carbonation bubble making a break for the top of the bottle!

If you purchase a bottle of coconut water kefir, you can create more Kefir in your kitchen with raw coconut water. If your coconut water is fresh out of a Coco Jacked coconut, simply strain it through a fine filter, then place in a glass jar, preferably a dark colored jar, but clear will work fine as well.

Add about ¼ cup (60ml) of coconut water kefir to about 2 cups (500ml) of raw coconut water and lightly stir. Keep it in an air tight jar, out of the sunlight, at room temperature. The probiotics in the Kefir will eat up the sugars in the coconut water and multiple. Depending on the temperature of your room, it will take between 24-48 hours for the coconut water to be fully converted into Kefir. You can test it every 6-8 hours by scooping a little bit out on a spoon and tasting it. Once the sweetness has completely transformed into sourness, you can place it in your refrigerator and it where it will be good for at least one week.

Charmed Chili Stack

160

Savvy Savory

Pumpkin CinnaBun

Sweet Rolls

162

Breakfast in Bed

Clever Condiments & Breakfast Bites

Pumpkin CinnaBun Sweet Rolls

When these Sugar-Free, Grain-Free CinnaBun Sweet Rolls are in the oven, it beckons everyone into the kitchen! The prospect of devouring a warm, ooey, gooey JingSmacked CinnaBun coupled with a cold JingNog, makes every day a holiday!

Gather Up

Dough
¾ cup (180ml) Water, warmed
2¼ tsp Active Dry Yeast
2 cups (250g) Otto's Cassava Flour
½ cup (65g) Arrowroot Flour
1½ tsp Psyllium Husk Powder
1 tsp Sea Salt
¾ cup (180ml) Coconut Milk, warmed
½ cup (120ml) Pumpkin Puree
1 tsp Cinnamon
2 TB SuperFood Shortening
2½ TB Xylitol Powder
1 TB SugaVida (optional)
1 tsp Apple Cider Vinegar
½ tsp Vanilla Stevia

Filling
½ cup (100g) Xylitol Crystal or Powder
2 TB SugaVida (optional)
3 tsp Cinnamon
2 tsp SuperFood Shortening, Coconut Oil or Ghee, melted
1 TB Almond Flour
½ cup (58g) Pecans, chopped
½ cup (58) Walnuts, chopped

Icing
Ice with SuperFood Salted Caramel (page 76)

Jing It Up

(Dough)
2 tsp Maca Powder
1 tsp Chaga Powder

Sling It Up!

Pre-heat oven to 375°F/190°C. Prepare either a 12-inch (30cm) round, or a 10x13 inch (25x33cm) baking pan with coconut oil. In a large bowl, sift together the cassava flour, arrowroot flour, psyllium husk, salt and cinnamon.

In a separate small bowl, mix the yeast in the warm water to proof, until it starts become frothy. In another bowl, mix together the warmed coconut milk, pumpkin puree, SuperFood Shortening/or oil, xylitol powder, SugaVida, apple cider vinegar and vanilla stevia until well combined.

Add the yeast mixture to the wet mixture. Stir well. Next add the dry contents to the wet contents, stirring until you have a soft dough. Place the dough in well-coconut oiled bowl. Cover and let it rise until it doubles in size, about 1 to 1½ hours.

Next, place the dough on a 12.5x16 inch (32x40cm) sheet of parchment with another sheet of parchment over it. Use your hands to knead it. Shape into a 10x14 inch (25x35cm) rectangle. Using a rolling pin will make this easy.

Time to mix your filling! In a medium-sized bowl, combine all of the filling ingredients. Spread the filling over the dough, leaving a 1-inch margin all the way around. Using the parchment as leverage, from the 14-inch (35cm) side, roll the dough from one side to the other, sealing it by brushing the margin with a little water.

Cut the roll into eight even pieces and place them snuggly in the pan. Sprinkle with additional xylitol powder and cinnamon. Allow it to rise for another 45 minutes.

Bake at 375°F/190°C for about 35 minutes until golden brown. Allow it to cool down before topping with the SuperFood Salted Caramel. Enjoy these warm, or room temperature!

Quiche Me!

This is a Paleo Perfect Breakfast in Bed, or on the go, especially when served in the individual muffin papers. Eggs are often called, "the perfect food," they are anabolic and provide essential fats and protein, as well as liver detoxifying and beauty enhancing minerals like sulfur. Pasture raised eggs contain important brain nutrients like choline and long chain omega-3 fatty acids like DHA. Jing Up your morning with a Quinton Hypertonic, adding in ocean trace minerals, or boost your immunity with some added chaga mushroom powder, which will add a slightly smoky flavor and plays nicely with the black truffle salt.

Gather Up

6 large Eggs
½ cup (120ml) Coconut Milk or Water
1 cup (30g) fresh Spinach Leaves or
Sunflower Sprouts
2 TB fresh Chives, chopped
2 TB Purple Onion, sliced

⅛ tsp Black Truffle Salt or Sea Salt
1 tsp Black Pepper
½ cup (50g) Manchego Sheep Cheese,
grated or Kite Hill Almond Truffle Cheese
½ tsp Garlic Granules

Jing It Up

1 Quinton Hypertonic
¼ tsp Chaga Powder

Sling It Up

Preheat Oven to 350°F/177°C. Prepare either a 12-cavity cupcake/ muffin pan with paper baking cups, an 8x8x3 inch (20x20x8 cm) baking dish, or a small cast iron skillet, lightly greased with coconut oil or ghee.

Mix all ingredients in a large bowl and whisk. Pour into baking cup papers in the cupcake/muffin pan, filling them ¾ full. If using the 8x8x3 inch (20x20x8 cm) baking dish, pour all of the quiche mixture into the pan. Place on the center of the middle rack in the oven and bake until puffed and lightly golden on top and firm to the touch, about 15-20 minutes.

Remove from oven and while still warm, top with extra cheese shreds and chives. Serve hot or keep them in a sealed container in the refrigerator for 7 days or freeze for up to 30 days. To reheat, simply pop them back in a 350°F/177°C oven until warmed through. For a delicious old-school quiche, pour this same recipe into our flakey pre-baked sugar-free, grain-free Savory Pie Crust (page 133), baking for the same timeframe.

"Quiche Me"

This Spaghetti Squash is the perfect upgrade for conventional potatoes and you'll **see** why, because they bring the antioxidants lutein and zeaxanthin to your breakfast table, which are known to bolster optimum healthy vision. These Hash Browns are perfect for any meal of the day, supplying your gut with beneficial fiber and lots of trace minerals to nourish your cells.

Gather Up

1 medium Spaghetti Squash, halved and seeded
1 medium Onion, sliced
½ tsp Black Pepper

½ tsp Black Truffle Salt or Sea Salt
½ tsp Garlic Granules
½ tsp All Purpose Seasoning
2 TB Coconut Oil

Jing It Up

½ tsp Astragalus Powder
½ tsp Chaga Powder
1 TB MCT Oil

Sting It Up

Pre-heat oven to 350°F/177°C.

Cut the spaghetti squash in half the long way, from stem to stern. Scoop out the seeds. You are going to want to seed save these seeds, as they easily grow in most climates, even right on your patio. Season the flesh with half of the spices and place flesh down on a parchment paper lined baking sheet. Bake in the center rack in your oven for about 35-40 minutes, until fork tender.

Remove from the oven and scoop the flesh out into a hot skillet with coconut oil and the sliced onions.

Sauté the remaining spices and the Jing It Up options with the onions, until the desired Hash Brown texture is reached.

Garnish with chives and shredded carrots. Serve with our KickAss Ketchup (page 174).

Pancakes are all about lazy weekend mornings and breakfast in bed! This is a chocoholic's wish come true! Chaga powder will bolster your immunity and you can Jing Up your hormones with the maca powder. Bring them to a whole 'nother level by adding "I Love You Berry Much" Strawberry JingLato (page 108) between each layer and topping with Coconut Whipped Cream (page 74) as pictured below.

These pancakes flip easily from Paleo to Vegan. If you are making the Vegan version, the swap is simple. It is important to use the fine ground almond flour from Honeyville, otherwise the pancakes can be a little bit grainy.

Gather Up (Paleo)

2½ cups (315g) fine ground blanched Almond Flour
½ cup (65g) of Otto's Cassava Flour
¼ tsp Baking Soda
¼ tsp Baking Powder
⅛ tsp Sea Salt
3 TB Cacao Powder
3 TB Xylitol Powder, to taste
6 large Eggs

¾ cup (180ml) Coconut Milk
1 tsp Lemon Juice
½ tsp Vanilla Stevia
½ tsp Chocolate Stevia
¼ cup (60ml) Water
¼ cup (46g) Lily's Sugar Free Chocolate Chips
Ghee, SuperFood Shortening or Coconut Oil
for pan cooking

Jing It Up
(Paleo or Vegan)

2 tsp Maca Powder
1 tsp MCT Oil
1 tsp Chaga Powder or Restore the Jing

Sling It Up (Paleo)

In a medium bowl, sift and/or mix together the dry ingredients and then add the chocolate chips. In a separate bowl, or in your blender, blend together the water, eggs, lemon juice, coconut milk, stevia and vanilla extract until creamed and frothy. Add the liquid ingredients to the dry ingredients and mix well. Let it meld for a few minutes. The gluten-free flours are very thirsty flours and by allowing them to soak up moisture you get a better pancake.

Heat your skillet over medium to low heat with a heaping tablespoon of coconut oil, ghee, or SuperFood Shortening. Add about 2 tablespoons of pancake batter to the pan, we use an ice cream scoop and smooth them with a spoon so they are not dome shaped. If you have trouble flipping the pancakes, try making them smaller about 3-4 inches wide. A wide, super-thin blade on the spatula is the secret to flipping these successfully.

Cook the pancake until it starts to bubble and the edges just start to brown up then you can flip. These cook quickly! Flip carefully. You can keep the pancakes in a warm oven until ready to serve. We like to make them ahead of time, freeze them and put them in the oven on a parchment lined sheet pan to reheat.

Sling It Up (Vegan)

All the ingredients and blending instructions remain the same except you will delete the eggs/ghee and increase the coconut milk to 1½ cups, the water to ½ cup and add in ¼ cup melted coconut oil into the wet ingredients when blending. These will be spooned onto a parchment lined sheet pan, smoothed into the pancake size and thickness you want. Bake in the oven at 375°F/191°C for about 25 minutes. They should puff up a bit and be firm to the touch when finished. Bonus! They all can be done at the same time. They are too delicate to cook in a skillet but come out perfect on parchment.

Maca Chocolate Pancakes

Pretty in Pink Pitaya Bowl

Pitaya (dragon fruit) contains oligosaccharides, specific sugars that feed the beneficial bacteria in our gut. The oligosaccharides in dragon fruit have been shown to feed both lactobacilli and bifidobacteria probiotics. The brilliant magenta color in pitaya comes from phenol antioxidants called betacyanins, which are the same compounds that give beetroots their dark red color. This creamy, nutrient dense breakfast bowl served in a fresh cantaloupe, delights both children and adults alike.

Gather Up

4 packets (100g each) frozen Pitaya
¼ cup (60ml) Coconut Milk
¼ cup (30g) Raspberries,
fresh or frozen
2 TB Collagen Powder, Whey Protein or
Vanilla Vegan Protein
¼ cup (38g) raw Cashews

1 TB Xylitol Powder
¼ tsp Vanilla Stevia
1 small Cantaloupe or
Honeydew Melon (optional as bowl)
Styrian Pumpkin Seeds
(optional garnish)
Hemp Seeds (optional garnish)

Jing It Up

½ TB Miracle Reds
1 TB Arnox Advantage
½ tsp Pure Radiance

Sling It Up

To prepare the bowl, cut the melon in half and scoop out the seeds. Cut a small slice from the rounded bottom to provide a flat surface to steady your live fruit bowl.

Run the pitaya packets under room temperature water for 3-5 seconds, break into 4-6 pieces and cut them open. Pour the coconut milk into blender, along with the rest of the ingredients and blast on high, blending with tamper if necessary, until smooth. If your blender does not have a tamper, add additional coconut milk until it blends smoothly.

Spoon into center of melon and dress with fruits, nuts and seeds of your choice.

KickAss Ketchup

This is a caring condiment, free of the conventional chemicals and GMO additives that age you before your time. Our JingSlinger KickAss Ketchup boosts a concentration of the beauty antioxidant lycopene and another optional antioxidant heavyweight in acai powder.

Gather Up

7 oz (200g) Tomato Paste (1 jar)
2 tsp Raw Apple Cider Vinegar, to taste
1 TB Xylitol Powder
1 tsp Dijon Mustard
1 TB Water

½ tsp Black Truffle Salt or Sea Salt
¼ tsp Garlic Granules
⅛ tsp Chili Chipotle, ground
⅛ tsp Black Pepper Powder
A Pinch of Cinnamon, to taste

Jing It Up

1 tsp Acai Powder

Sling It Up

Mix all ingredients together in a bowl and enjoy! You can definitely make it more spicy, or play with any of the flavors. This will keep for a very long time in the refrigerator, so you can mix up a double or triple batch and store it, to save kitchen time.

Dressed To Thrill Goji Balsamic

The Goji Berry elevates this dressing from ordinary to extraordinary. This premiere anti-aging Yin Jing Herb, builds blood, tonifies the liver and kidneys and tunes up your eyesight. This adaptogenic powerhouse balances you and supports healthy cellular function.

Gather Up

½ cup (120ml) Balsamic Vinegar
2 TB Goji Berries, soaked plump
1-2 TB Xylitol, SugaVida or
Raw Honey (to taste)
1¼ cup (370ml) Olive Oil
1 TB Water, (from Soaked Goji Berries)

1 tsp Lemon Juice
½ cup (12g) Fresh Basil,
chopped
and tightly packed
¼ tsp Ground Black Pepper
½ tsp Sea Salt

Jing It Up

2 tsp Pearl Powder
¼ tsp Astragalus Powder

Sling It Up

The goji berries needs to be rehydrated for this recipe to really deliver all of its adaptogenic properties. Simply place the dried goji berries into just enough warm water to cover the berries, soak for 10 minutes to plump and then drain. Save one tablespoon of the soak water for the dressing (and throw the remainder into your morning smoothie.) Place all ingredients into your blender except for half of the chopped basil. Blend on a medium speed until creamy. Hand stir in the remaining basil and the dressing is ready to serve!

Down On The Ranch

This is a 2-for-1 bonus recipe. Make our SuperFood "Down on the Ranch" Dressing by using our "Mac'N on the Qi'Z" sauce (page 194) for your base. In this recipe, to achieve that mouth watering "umani" flavor, the black truffle salt is a must.

Gather Up

½ cup (120ml) Mac'N on the Qi Z Sauce
½ cup (120ml) Coconut, Cashew or Almond Milk
¼ tsp Fresh Ground Black Pepper

¼ tsp Black Truffle Salt
¼ cup (60ml) Water

Sling It Up

Blend all ingredients in your blender adding additional water or Milk of choice until it is a dressing consistency.

Panini Perfecto

Outside the Lunchbox

Soups, Salads, Snacks & Sides

Silken Kabocha Bisque

Gather Up

1 TB Coconut Oil
½ cup (75g) Onion, diced
2 cups (500g) Kabocha Squash, baked
1½ cup (375ml) Water
2 cups (500ml) Coconut Milk
2 tsp (packed) Fresh Rosemary, chopped
(leaves, no stems)
1 tsp Black Truffle Salt or Sea Salt
1 tsp Black Pepper
1 tsp Garlic Granules
Spiced, Shelled Pumpkin Seeds (optional garnish)
Styrian Pumpkin Seed Oil (optional garnish)

Jing It Up

1 TB Ghee
1 tsp Chaga Powder
1 tsp Maca Powder
2 tsp Pearl Powder
2 TB Collagen Powder

Sling It Up

Pre-heat oven 365°F/185. Cut the squash in half. Remove the seeds and then sprinkle the flesh with black pepper, black truffle salt and garlic granules. Bake it (flesh down, skin on) on a parchment lined sheet pan until fork tender, about 30-45 minutes.

While it is baking, sauté the onion with the coconut oil and a pinch of truffle salt and black pepper in the bottom of a soup pot (which will ultimately hold the whole soup) until fork tender/translucent. Once cooked, transfer to your blender/food processor. A high performance blender works best.

Once the squash is cooked, scoop the flesh from the skin. Add the two packed cups of squash to your blender and one cup of the water along with the coconut milk, rosemary and spices. Save the half-cup of water to use for smoother blending, if needed. When using a blender, put a towel over the vented lid and blend at a low speed, gradually increasing the speed. Blend on a medium setting until smooth. Add additional salt and pepper to taste.

Pour the contents back into the soup pot to warm. Thin with additional coconut milk and water if a thinner consistency is desired.

(optional) Serve with a swirl of pumpkin seed oil and coconut milk on top, and garnish with whole shelled, spiced pumpkin seeds (sold in bags at Whole Foods) and a sprinkle of truffle salt.

Yields about six, one cup (250ml each) servings.

Soup has always been a favorite comfort food, especially when there is a chill in the air. A cup of soup warms your hands and your heart. These soups have both flavor and function. Kabocha contains naturally occurring beneficial pectins, which are polysaccharides that have been shown to have anti-inflammatory and even blood sugar balancing properties. This SuperHero Squash is known around the world for its aphrodisiac effects, however, a chic cheat for this recipe is to swap out the two cups of fresh Kabocha for two cups of frozen butternut squash.

Our "Faster Than Drive-Through Blender Basil Bisque" is in your pie-hole in mere minutes! Perfect for when you are on the go, or in need of a quick refrigerator veggie drawer clean out. But don't let the need for speed fool you, this soup boasts big beauty bonuses. The major antioxidant in tomatoes is lycopene. Lycopene is an anti-wrinkle avenger that inhibits the enzymes known as collagenases which break down the collagen in your skin.

Faster Than Drive-Through
Blender Basil Bisque

Gather Up

1 cup (210g, about 1 large) Avocado, peeled and pitted
4 cups (700g) Grape Tomatoes
2 cloves Garlic
¼ cup (10g) packed Fresh Basil (leaves, no stems)
½ cup (120ml) Coconut Milk
1 TB Olive Oil
⅛ tsp Black Truffle Salt or Sea Salt
⅛ tsp Black Pepper
Water as needed to blend to desired thickness

Jing It Up

1 tsp MCT Oil
½ tsp Acai Powder
½ tsp Maqui Powder
½ tsp Maca Powder
1 tsp Pearl Powder

Sling It Up

Blend all ingredients together on high speed, adding just enough water for desired soup consistency. Serve it right from the blender, the longer you blend it, the warmer it becomes. Garnish with microgreens, pine nuts or whatever you have in your fridge or pantry. Freestyle it, this is a fast one!

Antioxidants aren't the only gift that pomegranates have up their sleeve, they are well-known for having a tonifying effect on the heart, because they help to raise the body's level of nitric oxide, the signaling molecule for vasodilation. Spoon into shot glasses as a fun party appetizer or serve as a first course at a special holiday dinner in a martini glass.

Gather Up

2 cups (174g) Pomegranate Arils (seeds)
2 cups (450g) Orange Segments, peeled & seeded
½ cup (120ml) Orange Juice
1 TB Orange Zest
2 cups (450g) fresh Pears, cubed
1 cup (125g) Walnuts, rough chopped

Jing It Up

1 tsp Pearl Powder

Sling It Up

Toss all of the ingredients into a large bowl and stir. Cover and chill so the flavors meld.

Pomegranate Salad

Ribbon Salad

This simple salad is visually stunning with ribbons of brightly colored raw organic veggies. Pair it with the Dressed to Thrill Goji Balsamic Dressing (page 175), it is as bioavailable as it is beautiful. You can spiralize any raw veggies you wish, we list our favorites (pictured) for both fabulous flavor and physiological function. (Our favorite spiralizer is the Joyce Chen.) Gather up one spiralized vegetable for every two servings.

Gather Up

Rainbow Carrot
Watermelon Radish
Beet Root
Zucchini
Daikon Radish
Arugula
Butter Lettuce
Red Cabbage

Sling It Up

Wash all the veggies and peel the beetroot. The remaining veggies don't require being peeled. Spiralize the rainbow carrots, watermelon radish, beetroot, zucchini and daikon. Serve the veggie ribbons on the butter lettuce, red cabbage and arugula. Jing It Up with our Goji Balsamic Dressing!

Immortal Gut

Great tasting fermented vegetables? That's right! When we make this dish for parties, it is the first one gone. Powdered probiotic supplements are great, but nothing beats live probiotics in fermented foods. Naturally fermented dishes like Sauerkraut and Kim Chi can have *trillions* of beneficial bacteria in every serving, helping to keep your digestive and immune systems in top form.

These beneficial bacteria have predigested the vegetable fiber, so you get greater absorption of the vitamins in these vegetables because they are much more bioavailable. People who have candida overgrowth issues or immune challenges, should start slowly with just a few bites of fermented vegetables each day. The power of these vegetables are that they can be incredibly cleansing. A healthy person, however, can enjoy large amounts right off the bat. You can use a wide variety of Sauerkraut or Kim Chi flavors for this dish. If you live in the United States, our absolute favorite is the Smoked Jalapeño Sauerkraut from Farmhouse Culture. Our favorite nutritional yeast is from Quantum Nutrition Labs, because it is grown on molasses, which is a non-GMO medium.

Gather Up

2 cups (454g) Fermented Vegetables
⅓ cup (30g) Pumpkin Seeds, ground
½ cup (30g) Nutritional Yeast

¼ cup (60ml) Coconut Milk
½ tsp Yellow Curry Powder
½ tsp Fajita Seasoning

Jing It Up!

2 TB Styrian Pumpkin Seed Oil
2 tsp Mucuna Extract
1-2 tsp Sriracha Sauce

Sling It Up

Powderize the pumpkin seeds in a clean spice or coffee grinder. Add all the ingredients in a large bowl and mix together well. The final consistency will be similar to coleslaw. Store it in the refrigerator in an airtight container. It will stay good up to a week. Plain sauerkraut, properly sealed, will last a VERY long time in the fridge.

Gauc Star

This Guac Star sings in perfect harmony with this symphony of body boosting ingredients. Your skin and hormones get the best seats in the house for this South Florida inspired SuperHero Dip. We use Ninja Squirrel Sriracha in our Guacamole for the flavor and their clean ingredients, including less than one gram of sugar per serving.

Gather Up

4 Hass Avocados, peeled and pitted
1 Lemon, juice and zest
1 Lime, juice and zest
2 small Heirloom Tomatoes, diced
⅓ cup (50g) chopped Red Onion
1 cup (165g) diced Mango
(1 small ripe mango)

1 tsp Ninja Squirrel Sriracha
¼ tsp Chipotle Powder
½ tsp Garlic Granules
½ tsp Cumin
¼ tsp Ground Black Pepper
Sea Salt to taste

Jing It Up

1 tsp Maca
1 TB Fresh Cilantro, minced
1 Quinton HyperTonic
1 tsp Astragalus

Sling It Up

Place the peeled and pitted avocado and the remaining prepared ingredients into a large bowl and mash with a large fork or potato masher. Mix in any Jing It Up options and serve with plantain chips or sweet potato chips. Our favorite chips are from Jackson's Honest, shown on pages 202 & 204. They are organic, heirloom sweet potato and purple potato chips cooked in coconut oil (No rancid polyunsaturated fats! Yeah!). We also use the Guac Star as a layer in our Charmed Chili Stack (page 204).

Glowing Green Goddess Dressing

Easily flip your Guac Star into a Glowing Green Goddess Dressing (but don't let the name fool you, it's equally good for men or women). If you like creamy salad dressing, this, along with our Down on the Ranch Dressing (page 175) will satisfy every time. The base foods and herbs that are already in the Guac Star, paired with extra Jing It Up Tonic Herbal uplifters, make this is a functional salad dressing with a purpose!

Gather Up

½ cup (100g) Guac Star
¼ cup (60ml) Coconut Milk, Cashew Milk or Almond Milk
2 TB Fresh Arugula, packed tight
2 TB Olive Oil
¼ cup (60ml) Water, plus more if needed.

Jing It Up

¼ tsp Astragalus Powder
¼ tsp Ashwagandha Powder
¼ tsp Maca Powder
2 tsp Pearl Powder

Sling It Up

Blend all ingredients in your blender adding additional water or milk of choice until it is a dressing consistency.

Panini Perfecto

Quick Coconut Flour Flatbread

This is a Vegan & Paleo 1-bowl, 1-spoon recipe that takes mere minutes to make! With all the benefits that coconut brings to your plate, plus hormone boosting with a blast of maca, who could ask for more from your sandwich? Freestyle with this adaptogenic bread, as it will make a grilled Panini sandwich (facing page) as easily as a flatbread appetizer for unexpected guests. Recipe yields 4-6 flatbreads.

Gather Up

½ cup (65g) Coconut Flour
2 TB Psyllium Husk Powder
¼ cup (60g) Coconut Oil, melted
2 tsp Fresh Rosemary Leaves, minced (no stems)

½ tsp Garlic Granules
⅛ tsp Black Pepper
⅛ tsp Sea Salt
1 cup (250ml) Water, boiling

Jing It Up

1 tsp Maca Powder
1 tsp MCT Oil

Sling It Up

Put all the dry ingredients into a bowl. Stir with a spoon until it is well mixed. Add the melted coconut oil into the mixture and stir in the boiling water as you pour it in. Once mixed and cool enough to handle (just a few seconds), hand roll into a ball, then split the ball into four or six equal pieces.

On a piece of parchment paper, individually flatten each quarter into a flat disk, either by hand, or with a rolling pin and a second piece of parchment paper, so that the disk is about ⅛ inch thick. Using our hands is our method.

Use your favorite skillet, or crepe pan. You can use no oil or you can very lightly spray/oil with either ghee or coconut oil. Put the pan on medium heat. Drop the disks into the pan one at a time, cook until it is lightly browned on one side, then flip and lightly brown on the opposite side. A super thin spatula makes it easy to flip.

This flatbread is both flavorful and flexible and can be made in a hot pan with NO oil, but you need to watch it like a hawk so it does not burn or stick, as without the oil it can do both quickly!

Flatbreads will stay fresh in the refrigerator in a sealed container/bag for 3-5 days. They freeze beautifully up to 30 days. Can be made into pizza, sandwiches, panini, gyros, pita, etc.

Now you can make the Panini of your dreams! Sling it however you like. As pictured on the left, we made it with Kite Hill Almond Ricotta and Truffle Dill Cheeses with tomatoes, caramelized onions and spinach. Topped with Goji Balsamic Dressing (page 175).

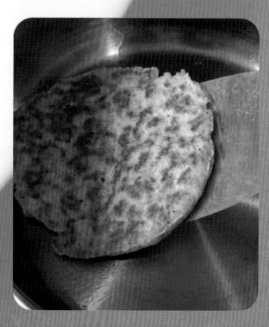

GlowTatoes

Cauliflower makes this mash a winner, no nightshade aches from these taters! Creamed with coconut milk, herbs and spices, they delight your taste buds, quell your comfort food cravings and make both your belly and your cells very happy. Use it for a killer Shepherd's Pie or to make GlowTato Pancakes for breakfast, just JingSmack with minced chives and give them a fast flip in your skillet.

Gather Up

I large Cauliflower
½ cup (120ml) Coconut Milk
4-6 Cloves Roasted Garlic
3 TB Ghee or SuperFood Shortening
¼ tsp Black Truffle Salt or Sea Salt (to taste)
¼ tsp Fresh Ground Black Pepper (to taste)

Jing It Up

½ tsp Chaga
1 tsp Pearl
1 TB MCT Oil

Sling It Up

Preheat oven 350°F/177°C.

For the roasted garlic, simply cut the top point off of a whole garlic bulb thus exposing the tops of the cloves. Drizzle with MCT oil and a pinch of sea salt. Wrap in parchment paper and then wrap in tin foil and place in the oven at 350°F/177°C for 30 minutes or until soft.

Cut the cauliflower into bite-sized pieces and steam until very tender, soft to the touch. Toss all of the ingredients into your food processor, except for the coconut milk and spin it until it is well incorporated. Then add the coconut milk, a splash at a time until you get smooth mashed potato consistency. Taste for spice tweaking, or for extra ghee or coconut milk.
We always finish with more black truffle salt for a deeper umami yum factor.

Slinging Supper

Italian, Indian, and South of the Border

Flatbread 101 & Pizza
190

Heart Beet Rawvioli
200

Sweet Potato Naan
192

Charmed Chili
202

Mac'N on the Qi'Z
194

South Beach Salsa
205

Zoodles
195

Quinoa Risotto
206

Blender Marinara
197

JingSmacked Kitchari
208

Gratitouille
198

JingSlinger Blender FlatBread

This Grain-Free Crust gives you a ton of healthy options! This is our favorite "batch day cooking" Pizza Crust/Flatbread. You can have Pizza, Panini & Flatbreads ready to go in your fridge or freezer all week long. This has built-in Jing, with the psyllium husk for digestion and the coconut meat and MCT oil for fat burning and immunity. Top this with our Probiotic Ricotta Almond Cheese after it comes out of the oven for a real SuperHero Pizza!

Gather Up

2 cups (454g) Raw Young Thai Coconut Meat (page 158)
½ cup (180ml) Coconut Milk
2 TB Fresh Rosemary Leaves, no stems
½ cup (75g) Raw, Chopped Onion
1 TB Minced Garlic

¾ cup (95g) Cassava Flour or your favorite GF Flour
2 TB Psyllium Husk Powder
2 TB MCT Oil
½ cup (120ml) Water
½ tsp Black Truffle Salt or Sea Salt
½ tsp ground Black Pepper

Sling It Up

Preheat your oven to 365°F/ 185°C, line a large sheet pan or cookie sheet with parchment paper. Add all the ingredients into a high performance blender or split the recipe in half and blend in batches as it is a thick batter for a conventional blender to handle. Blend all the ingredients until smooth and a thick batter forms.

This is a sticky batter! Distribute the batter to form either 1 large rectangular pizza crust, 2 medium round or square crusts, or 4 personal sized crusts, smoothing with an offset spatula or with wet or oiled fingers, so that the crust is uniformly about ¼ - ½ inch thick.

Sprinkle with sea salt, garlic granules and/or Italian seasoning and bake until evenly browned on the top and the bottom of the crust. Baking time varies with different ovens, about 45 – 90 minutes. It bakes faster with a convection oven.

Once the crust is fully cooked, add the toppings you wish and cook until your toppings are done to your liking. Cut and serve. This crust freezes and reheats in the oven beautifully. To the right you can see two medium round flatbreads being spread. The large background picture is the big family-sized rectangle crust right out of the oven and ready to dress. Our Blender Marinara is on page 197, the Probiotic Ricotta Almond Cheese and the Basil Pesto are waiting for you on page 200.

Sweet Potato Naan

Three ingredient SuperFood Naan! These beta-carotene rich Grain-Free Naan rounds double as yummy wraps or tortillas. Switch up the spices for either a sweet or savory bread or crust. The water content of the sweet potato is uber important. Therefore, the raw sweet potatoes MUST be steamed and not baked, to create the mash. These Naan remain soft and pliable for sandwiches, wraps or add a sliced baked apple for an apple pie on the fly!

Gather Up

2 cups (500g) Sweet Potato, steamed & mashed
2 cups (250g) Cassava Flour

1 TB Psyllium Husk Powder
¼ tsp Cinnamon or Cumin (optional)
Pinch of Sea Salt

Sling It Up

Place two whole, unpeeled medium-sized sweet potatoes in a covered pot, fitted with a steamer basket. Do not allow the sweet potatoes to sit in the water, steam until fully fork tender. Once tender, slide the peels off while they are still hot and mash with a fork in a medium-sized bowl. While still hot, quickly mix in the rest of your ingredients until it forms a soft dough.

With floured hands and on parchment paper, roll into a log shape and divide into six even sections. With your hands, form each section into a round disk. One by one roll out each disk into a ¼ inch thick, round tortilla. Place the finished tortilla into a deep dish or bowl, lined and covered by two clean dish towels to maintain warmth. Stack each tortilla on top of the last one in the bowl, until all six are completed and remain covered.

Heat a skillet or crepe pan over medium heat. Using a coconut oil spray, very lightly spray your pan. Cook each flatbread, one at a time, flipping each one every 30 seconds. They may balloon up as the heat releases the steam, after the second flip. Keep flipping them until they are cooked through and still pliable. (This takes a few flips on each side, depending on how wet your sweet potatoes were). If they are sticking, adjust your heat accordingly.

Keep them warm by stacking them as each is finished in the same towel-lined bowl. They are now ready to eat and they freeze beautifully for later use. They will keep in the refrigerator in a sealed container for 5-7 days.

Mac'N on the Qi'Z

Everybody loves Macaroni and Cheese! This Vegan and Paleo favorite can be Slung Grain-Free in minutes by simply choosing your favorite noodle. Our Dairy-Free JingSlinger béchamel cheese sauce brings to the table branch chain amino acids for muscle repair, glutathione for detoxification and beneficial probiotics in the Cultured Almond Cheeses. Our Jing It Up options offer hormone stability and fat burning brain food.

Gather Up

1 cup (224g) Kite Hill
Almond Ricotta Cheese
1 cup (224g) Kite Hill
Almond Cream Cheese with Chives
½ cup (30g) Quantum Nutrition Labs
Nutritional Yeast
1 tsp Dijon Mustard

½ tsp Styrian Pumpkin Seed Oil
1 tsp Ninja Squirrel Sriracha
½ tsp Coconut Aminos
½ tsp Paprika
½ tsp Black Ground Pepper
½ tsp Garlic Granules
½ tsp Black Truffle Salt or Sea Salt

Jing It Up

½ tsp Maca Powder
1 tsp MCT Oil
Quinton Hypertonic
⅛ tsp Turmeric Powder

Sling It Up

To create the dairy-free béchamel for your Mac and Cheese, add all your ingredients into your blender and blend until smooth, adding a little additional water for desired thickness. Tweak any of the spices to your liking.

Pour over your favorite gluten-free noodles. Our favorite pasta to use it "Tru Roots" brand elbows. It is gluten & sugar-free. For our grain-free Paleo friends, spiralized Zucchini Noodles (Zoodles), Cappello's Fettuccini, Miracle Noodles, or Sea Tangle Kelp Noodles work great as a macaroni stand-in. Learn how to flip this sauce into our "Down on the Ranch" Dressing on page 175.

Zucchini Noodles (Zoodles)

1 medium raw zucchini per person (Spiral cut into noodles, as pictured on the next page).

To make the raw zucchini noodles cut the ends off of two straight, fat zucchini (curvy zucchini don't work as well for long noodles). You may peel the green skins off or leave them on. Place one on the spiral cutter (we use the Paderno World Cuisine Tri-Blade Spiral Vegetable Slicer) and spin the handle with even pressure. Noodles in no time!

Toss with the Mac'N on the Qi'Z sauce, add a sprinkle of pine nuts if desired and enjoy one of the best comfort foods ever!

Oodles of Zoodles!

JingMaster Blender Marinara

This SuperFood Sauce is ready right out of the blender, but you will get more depth of flavor and a bigger kick of the lycopene when you turn on the heat! Marinara warming on the stove not only makes the house smell amazing , it also boosts the antioxidant bioavailability. It also brings out the best in the Jing It Up tonic herbs. Add a Quinton Hypertonic vial to boost your micronutrients from a super clean ocean source.

Gather Up

2 cups (454g) Sundried Tomatoes (packed in Olive Oil)
2 cups (500ml) Glen Muir Fire Roasted Crushed Tomatoes
1 pint/ basket (340g) Heirloom Cherry/ Grape Tomatoes
½ cup (21g) packed Fresh Basil (leaves, no stems)
1 TB Minced Garlic
Sea Salt & Black Pepper, to taste
1 TB Italian/Pizza Seasoning (your favorite)
1 TB Olive Oil
Water as needed to blend to desired thickness

Jing It Up

⅛ tsp Reishi
⅛ tsp Astragalus
⅛ tsp Restore the Jing
1 tsp Acai Berry Powder
1 tsp Maqui Berry Powder
1 vial Quinton HyperTonic

Sling It Up

Add all items to your high speed blender or food processor and blend until smooth on high setting which will heat it as it blends for a hot meal in minutes. Pour over raw zucchini "Zoodles" for a fast Gluten-Free pasta dinner. Enjoy!

Italian Meatballs, Spicy Italian Sausage, Lasagna, Pizza and Manicotti are all possible with this versatile Vegan SuperHero Recipe. We've had hardcore Italian Omnivores shocked out of their shoes that the lasagna they just ate was meatless. We always make this in larger batches because it freezes so well and can be ready any night of the week. It is an antioxidant and lycopene lift-off!

Gather up

1½ cups (175g) Walnuts, soaked
1½ cups (175g) Pecans, soaked
1 cup (225g) Olive Oil packed Sundried Tomatoes
¾ cup (30g) Packed Fresh Basil Leaves, no stems
¼ cup (20g) Freshly ground Fennel Seeds + 1 tsp
¼ cup (60ml) Olive Oil (from the Sundried Tomatoes or Olive Oil of your choosing)
3 Medium raw Garlic Cloves, minced fine
2 tsp Italian Seasoning (your favorite brand)
2 tsp Garlic Granules
1 tsp Fresh ground Black Pepper
1 tsp Sea Salt
1 cup (150g) Zucchini, shredded
½ cup (30g) Carrots, shredded
¼ cup (38g) Onion, diced
7oz (200g) jar Tomato Paste
½ cup (112g) Glen Muir Fire-Roasted Crushed Tomatoes
3 TB Water (only if needed while processing the batches)

Jing It Up

1 tsp Acai Powder
1 tsp Chaga Powder
1 tsp Awaken the Shen
2 tsp Pure Synergy

To make as depicted, simply fill either Coconut Paleo Wraps or Gluten-Free lasagna sheets. Roll firmly, place in oven safe dish with your favorite sauce and heat at 350°F/177°C until warmed through. Serve over sautéed spinach and sprinkle with fresh basil and hemp seeds.

Gratitouille

Sling It Up

Finely grind all the fennel seeds in a spice or coffee grinder. Set aside. Soak walnuts and pecans with 1 teaspoon of the fennel seed powder and a pinch of sea salt for at least 2-4 hours or overnight. Discard the soak water, rinse well and drain.

Mince the zucchini, carrots and onions in a food processor, or finely chop. Sauté the zucchini, carrots and onions in a large pan with 2 tablespoons of olive oil and 2 minced cloves of garlic until they are all fork tender. Add the fire roasted crushed tomatoes to the pan and stir until all of it is warmed through. In the food processor, place the walnuts and pecans along with the basil, remaining olive oil, spices and sundried tomatoes and pulse until it is the consistency of coarse wet sand.

In a large bowl, transfer the nut mixture, all the cooked vegetables and any of the remaining ingredients, including the Jing It Up options and stir with a large spoon until uniformly combined. Place a half or a third of this mixture into the food processor at a time and blend in batches to the consistency of paté. Put all of the final Gratitouille batches back in the large bowl and mix together. Now you can roll it into balls, stuff gluten-free wraps or sheet pasta for manicotti, fill rice papers to make a sausage, layer between thin zucchini slices for a kick-ass lasagna or layer it for a torta with our Almond Cheese Ricotta and Basil Pesto (next page).

Raw, Vegan and Paleo dinner in minutes without the oven or stovetop!! This ravioli pumps up your Nitric Oxide levels to support a healthy heart and circulation. Nobel Laureate in Medicine Dr. Louis Ignarro explained that by boosting the nitric oxide levels our body we can prevent and even reverse heart disease. Beets are one of the top foods that deliver this protection. The "Pasta" is thinly sliced raw beet, with a 30-minute quick marinate in olive oil and spices. Choose your favorite filling and dinner is served.

Gather Up

(for Pasta)
2 large raw beets, peeled
¼ cup Olive Oil
¼ tsp Black Truffle Salt or Sea Salt
¼ tsp Garlic Granules

(for Pesto)
2 cups Fresh Basil Leaves, packed tight
¾ cups Pine Nuts or Pistachios, toasted
5 TB Extra Virgin Olive Oil
1 TB MCT Oil

½ tsp Sea Salt or Black Truffle Salt
¼ tsp Fresh ground Black Pepper
1 tsp Maca Powder
1 tsp Lemon Juice

Almond Cheese Filling

1 cup (227g) Kite Hill Almond Ricotta Cheese or
Homemade Nut Cheese Option*
2 cups (200g) Pine Nuts, soaked
3 TB Nutritional Yeast
2 TB Lemon Juice

¼ tsp Garlic Granules
½ tsp Sea Salt
¼ tsp Fresh Ground Black Pepper
4-6 TB (90ml) Coconut Milk
Probiotic Powder, from 3 opened capsules

Sling It Up

Peel the beet and slice on the thinnest setting of your mandoline. Using a heart-shaped cookie cutter, cut each beet slice by simply pressing down on the slice, one at a time, with the sharp edge of the cookie cutter. Toss the beet hearts in the olive oil and spices in a small bowl and allow to marinate in the refrigerator for at least 30 minutes, the longer the more tender.

Place all the pesto ingredients into your food processor and pulse adding the olive oil, one tablespoon at a time, until the pesto comes together, and set aside.

If you choose to buy the Kite Hill Almond Ricotta, just mix in a bowl with a splash of coconut milk, salt, pepper and garlic granules (to taste) until a thick spreadable cheese forms.

*If you choose to do the homemade recipe- *Soak the pine nuts for 1-hour, then discard the soak water.* **Place all prepared ingredients into your clean food processor except the coconut milk, and pulse while adding the milk one tablespoon at a time until a thick spreadable cheese forms. Taste and tweak spices as you wish.**

Goji Balsamic Dressing - see page 175
Gratitouille Optional Additional Filling - see page 198

Assembly and Serving: Place one heart-shaped beet on the plate, put a dollop of nut cheese, (a dollop of Gratitouille filling is optional but awesome here) and place the top heart-shaped beet over the fillings. Arrange the stuffed hearts on the serving plate and dress with the Pesto and Goji Balsamic. Garnish with spiralized carrots, beets and zucchini. These make great party appetizers too!

Heart Beet Rawvioli

Charmed Chili

This comfort food favorite welcomes everyone to the table. It has been overhauled by being more digestive friendly, reducing the nightshades and by adding antioxidant Jing It Up options. The rainbow of vegetables in this chili isn't the only thing that makes it so "charming." Fat burning MCT oil, gut soothing cooked celery and a whole bowl full of beta-carotenes disguised in our Charmed Chili makes it easy to get your kids to eat a whole array of vegetables.

Gather Up

2 TB MCT Oil or Ghee
2 TB Minced Garlic
1 cup (150g) Onions, chopped
1 cup (110g) Celery, fresh, chopped
2 cups (125g) Rainbow Carrots, sliced, fresh or frozen
2 cups (400g) Sweet Potato, cubed, fresh or frozen
2 cups (325g) Zucchini, cubed
3 cups (615g) Butternut Squash, cubed, fresh or frozen
3 cups (300g) Spinach, whole leaf, fresh or frozen

1 cups (101g) Rainbow Swiss Chard
1 tsp Chili Powder (or more to taste)
1½ TB Cumin Powder
½ tsp Chipotle Powder
1 tsp Sea Salt
1 TB Fajita Seasoning
2 tsp Granular Garlic
1 tsp Black Pepper
6 cups (1560g) Muir Glen Fire Roasted Tomatoes, diced
¾ cup (200gram) Tomato Paste
1 cup (250ml) Water, or Gynostemma Tea

Jing It Up

2 tsp Maca Powder
2 tsp Astragalus Powder
2 tsp Chaga Powder
1 TB Acai Powder

Sling It Up

In a large, heavy pot, heat the oil over medium-high heat. Add the onions, garlic, celery and carrots. Cook until fork tender. Add the sweet potato, zucchini and butternut squash. Add half a cup of water and half of all the spices, stirring until tender and the vegetables release their juices and start to caramelize. Add the remaining spices, the tomatoes, tomato paste, spinach and swiss chard. Add the remaining half cup of water, and stir well. Reduce the heat to simmer, stirring frequently, for about 30 minutes.

Adjust your seasoning, salt and pepper to taste. Continue to cook until all vegetables are fork tender. Add the Jing It Up herbs and simmer on a lower heat for an additional 20 minutes.

Paleo Option

2 pounds (906g) Ground Bison, or ¼ pound (113g) of Bison per serving

In a separate skillet, add 1 TB MCT oil or ghee, ½ cup diced onion, 1 TB minced fresh garlic, 1 tsp black pepper, 1 tsp black truffle salt (or sea salt) and cook until translucent, then add the ground bison. Sauté until cooked through. Add to individual bowls of chili while serving or you can add the bison to the entire pot of chili just before serving.

South Beach Salsa

With a Living Waters Margarita (page 142) in hand, this salsa is its BFF (Best Friend Forever!) Lycopene and carotenoids start your engines! This salsa has antioxidant properties, the detoxifying chemistry of chlorophyll and cilantro to send heavy metals packin'. Upright Qi energy from astragalus and deep ocean plasma minerals from the Quinton or sea salt to balance your inner ocean.

Gather Up

4 Medium Heirloom Tomatoes, Roma Tomatoes or
2 pints Cherry Tomatoes, diced
⅓ cup (50g) Red Onion, chopped
1 cup (165g) Mango, diced
(or 1 small ripe mango)
1 TB Fresh Cilantro, minced

1 Lime, juice and ½ the zest
1 tsp Fresh Jalapeño, diced
¼ tsp Chipotle Powder
½ tsp Garlic Granules
½ tsp Cumin
¼ tsp Ground Black Pepper
Sea Salt to taste

Jing It Up

1 tsp Maca Powder
1 Quinton Vial
1 tsp Astragalus Powder
½ tsp Chloroxygen

Sling It Up

Mix all the prepared ingredients in a bowl, stir and allow to marinate about 30 minutes in the refrigerator before serving.

How To Sling a Chili Stack 101

This is a simple trick that makes a beautiful presentation. All you need is the ring (to make your own, cut the bottom and top out of a metal coconut milk so that it becomes a tube, or ring.) Next, have your "layers" ready to go. "Mise en Place," cooked Purple Forbidden Rice, Guac Star, Charmed Chili and South Beach Salsa. Lightly spray coconut oil inside the ring and place it on a flat dish with a flattened cupcake paper under the base. The oil will allow the perfect release later and the paper allows you to move it to the plate for serving flawlessly.

Spoon in a layer of the rice and tamp down with a spoon to compact the rice as a stable base. A small juice glass that fits down into the ring works great for both compacting and for the steady gentle release when plating. Next add the chili and press into place, then pack the Guac Star and the Salsa as the next layers. Chill in the fridge on a plate to firm up. To get the stack out of the ring simply place on the serving plate, pull out the muffin paper, press down gently on the stack while lifting the ring until the stack is revealed. Garnish and serve!

Coconut Quinoa Risotto

Is it a grain? *Nah, Brah*, it's a SuperFood! Quinoa was a sacred, staple food of the Inca in South America and has been consumed for over 5,000 years. It is a complete protein food, containing all nine essential amino acids and contains a high amount of antioxidants such as the flavonoids quercetin and kaempferol. It has been shown to lower inflammation in adipose (fat) tissue and in the intestinal tract. Now you can have it creamy and drool-worthy in this renovated comfort food!

Gather Up

2 TB MCT Oil or Ghee
1 TB Minced Garlic
½ cup (150g) Onions, chopped
½ cup (55g) Celery, fresh, chopped
½ cup (125g) Carrots, shredded
1 cup (200g) Sweet Potato, cubed, fresh or frozen
1 cup (325g) Zucchini, cubed
2 cups (410g) Butternut Squash, cubed, fresh or frozen
1 TB Fresh Basil Leaves, chiffonade

1 cup (300g) Spinach, whole leaf, fresh or frozen
½ tsp Black Truffle Salt or Sea Salt
½ tsp Garlic Granules
½ tsp Black Pepper
1 cups Button, Cremini or Baby Bella Mushrooms, sliced
2 cups (750ml) Vegetable Stock or Chicken Bone Broth
3 cups Coconut Milk
3 cups Quinoa, cooked

Jing It Up

3 TB Ghee
2 tsp Astragalus
2 tsp Lions Mane Powder

Sling It Up

Sauté the onions, mushrooms, celery, carrots and garlic, in MCT oil or ghee until tender with half of the salt, pepper and garlic granules. Add the sweet potatoes and then add one quarter, to one half of the vegetable stock/bone broth. Next, add the spinach, basil and butternut squash.

Once all the vegetables are fork tender, add the cooked quinoa, the remaining stock/bone broth and the remaining measured salt, pepper and garlic.

Finally, add the coconut milk, one cup at a time, stirring the Risotto until well-combined. If adding the ghee, stir it until melted and combined.

Let simmer on low heat until ready to serve.

** Risotto tends to become very thick, so to reheat it, add either additional vegetable stock/bone broth, coconut milk, water and/or ghee, without diluting the original creaminess. Reheat on low heat. Refrigerate for 2-4 days, otherwise it freezes and reheats like a champ.

JingSmacked Kitchari

In the United States today, juice fasting is one of the most popular forms of detoxification, but in Ayurveda, they use Kitchari, which is both cleansing and rejuvenating. Kitchari is a combination of white basmati rice and split yellow mung beans. Both of these foods are specifically good for each of the Ayurvedic Dosha (body) types. It is very easy to digest and is often given as the first food for infants as well as for people who are healing in the hospital. It can be made and enjoyed as a solo meal, or eaten as every meal for days or weeks at a time. This latter application gives rest to the digestive system and allows the body to detoxify.

We love to supercharge our Kitchari with tasty Jinged-Up SuperFoods! Astragalus for immunity and upright Qi force, mucuna for brain enhancement and a natural dopamine boost, and SugaVida for broad spectrum B Vitamin nutrition and amazing flavor.

People who have weak digestion can change the ratio of rice to beans to 2:1 or even 3:1, in favor of more rice. Split yellow mung beans are also sold as "dahl beans." Kitchari will last well in the refrigerator for 3-4 days. Reheat on a stove top or in your oven.

Gather up

1 cup (225g) dried White Basmati Rice
1 cup (225g) dried Split Yellow Mung Beans
8 cups (2000ml) Water
2 tsp Yellow Curry Powder
1 tsp Cumin Powder
½ tsp Garlic Powder

¼ Black Pepper Powder
¼ tsp Cardamon Powder
½ tsp Sea Salt
½ tsp Cinnamon Powder
1 Whole Carrot, grated
1 cup fresh greens, Spinach, Kale, etc
½ cup fresh Onion, diced
4 TB Ghee or SuperFood Shortening

Jing It Up

1 TB Mucuna Extract
1 TB SugaVida
1 TB Astragalus Powder

Sling it up

Pour the split yellow mung beans onto a baking sheet or flat surface and pick out any stray little stones. Soak the white basmati rice and split yellow mung beans together in a bowl, covered with at least an inch of water. Let them soak for a few hours, or even overnight. If you are in more of a hurry, you can boil the water, and soak them in the boiled water for an hour. In every case, discard the soak water.

In a separate pot on the stove, bring your 8 cups of water to a boil, then add the rice, beans, powdered spices and ghee (or SuperFood Shortening). Let it cook on a gentle boil for about 10 minutes, then bring it down to a simmer for another 15-25 minutes. Midway through the simmering process, add your fresh vegetable ingredients. If it is starting to stick on the bottom of the pan, add another ½ - 1 cup of water and reduce the heat. The final texture of your Kitchari will be soft, like a very soft porridge. You can customize the texture of the fresh vegetables however you prefer them, cook them more if you want them soft, cook them less if you want to have a little crunch left in them.

Spa Day Fun With Food!

The beautifying properties of our Bravocado are put into high definition when it is used topically as a Chocolate Facial Masque.

This puts more "fun" into functional food. Simply leave the stevia out of the recipe and slather it on! This is also a great way to save money with avocados that are starting to go south, by blending them into a soothing skin treatment.

Beyond
the
Plate...

Nature is always feeding us.

Sungazing at sunset sends the message to your brain to switch on the melatonin cascade for our natural sleep cycle chemistry.

That's why watching the sunset instead of the nightly news can literally help you relax into a better night's sleep! Our primal blueprint recognizes both the amber light in the evening to ready our bodies for sleep and the bright white/blue tone at dawn triggers the production of your morning cortisol.

The sun also bolsters our Vitamin D levels, a crucial fat-soluble nutrient which plays a role in numerous function in the body, including the absorption of minerals in our intestinal tract, our immune system, mood, and even the regulation of gene expression.

Acknowledgements

With Great Gratitude

"Food With Benefits" came to life because 499 KickStarter SuperFood SuperHeroes stepped up and supported this dream with their trust and their dollars. Grateful isn't a big enough word for the love we feel for every one of you. Our Deepest Gratitude goes out to all of our 499 KickStarter Angels! We literally could not have done this without you.

Your donations to reserve your piece of cookbook history with our FWB book, our digital JingSlinging 101 Class, or our Culinary Intensive and Teach & Taste Keynote rewards, has allowed us to deliver our important Evolved Eating message in a completely eco-green printed book. We know that blissful nutrient dense SuperFood meals build a sharp mind, a healthy body and a shining spirit. We were truly touched and humbled by the overwhelming response we received, and we are so incredibly grateful for everyone who contributed, shared our FWB campaign with others and rallied by our side with enthusiastic encouragement during this project!

A very Special Thanks to some remarkable JingMasters in Training - Jeff Skeirik, Justin Polgar, Lynne Sykes, Susan & Jay Nussbaum, Jim & Nancy Denman and Jaiya, you all supported this labor of love in so many different ways and every bit of this book reflects the guidance, support and wisdom you imparted.

Big Love to our JingSlinger Jedi in training - Keir Wohlman, Bob Zangrillo, Lorraine Taki, John & Kari Coelho, Laura Rush, Corey Kashiwagi, Rich & Annastasia Burright, Sophie Fletcher, Joannie & Eddie Rodrigues, Jill & Gregg Forgea, Jan and Michael Smith, Kaushi & Jerry Coelho, David & Pauline Gimbel, Mia Loewinger, Patrick Reardon, and Katherine & Shawn Mottram, we are delighted to watch you come into your own as JingSlingers.

Sincere Gratitude and Lots of Love to Dr. George Lamoureux, your incredible herbal expertise is only outshined by your generous and gracious heart, we are honored to call you friend. Jay Foster, you have saved and educated countless people, and it was you, Dr. Andrew Karp and David Avocado Wolfe who elevated Joy at the start of her journey that has become the important underpinnings of our JingMaster lifestyle. You are all the original Wellness Biohackers and we are eternally grateful for the wonderful work you continue to give to the world. Thank you to Rebecca Gauthier and Len Foley for inspiring and educating countless people every year with the LongevityNOW® Conference, which is where this all began for us together.

Big Love and Cosmic Hugs to Gabrielle Anwar, Stacy Keibler, Catherine Oxenberg, Ele Keats, Casper Van Dien, Dave Asprey, Ryan Carnes, and Matt & Agustina Picasso Groening, you have inspired so many of our Signature Recipes as Clever SuperHero Comfort Food to fuel you and your loved ones and we love you and thank you for your extremely important part of this dream.

Big Brother Steven... We Love You Steven Tyler! You spark inspiration in us daily, it is an honor to create new dishes that both delight and supercharge you, Aimee, AJ and your beautiful family, Namaste. You are a remarkable human, an original JingSlinger, a national treasure and a good-hearted friend.

Tess Masters, you are a true Force of Nature and we are so blessed to have your incredible energy in our lives. There are a thousand reasons why we love you and Scott, this book and our lives are better because you are in them both. You inspire and uplift so many people and we are so honored that you blessed this book with such heartfelt words. Thank you Sister Tess!

Jason Wrobel, you were a guiding light throughout our first cookbook adventure. You are an amazing chef, a great friend and we love you more than words can say... Thank You Brother Jason.

AnnaBlanca Teleky, our amazing SisterGirl Chocolate SuperHero, how do we find the words to properly Thank You?! This all started with this recipe... you, the Vortex that was the old school tonic bar, and your apartment. Thank you is not enough. There is a level of appreciation that cannot be conveyed with ink on paper. Know that we love you and we look forward to more Vortex Adventures with you and Sage.

These are the people who we appreciate madly, not just because they gave up a day to be part of one of our photo shoots, but because these wonderful humans are real, genuine friends who believe in us and the important message this project brings to the world. We are humbled by your love and support and we are elated that you "get" our science geek-ery and relentless pursuit of all things true, Thank You for that love - Grace Cavanaugh, Tommy Dale, Sage Dammers, Rich Enion, Ele Keats, Whitney Lauritsen, Jeff Skeirik, Mia Loewinger, Annablanca Teleky, and Jason Wrobel.

We respect and love these amazing companies and the incredible people who make them tick. They help us to educate, illuminate and elevate each person who stands before us. We love your beautiful intention and important message -

Addictive Wellness, Ancient Organics, Bulletproof, Bergman Family Chiropractic, Bliss River Podcast, Castle Rock Spring Water, Dragon Herbs, E3Live, Erewhon Market, Extreme Health Radio, Jing Herbs, Longevity Warehouse, Omica Organics, One Radio Network, Sexy Vegan Radio, SugaVida, Surthrival and Yes Cacao.

Eat, Drink & Glow,

Joy & Jay

Endnotes

SuperFoods

Acai
1) http://www.ncbi.nlm.nih.gov/pubmed/22137267
2) http://www.ncbi.nlm.nih.gov/pubmed/17061840

Aloe Vera
1) http://www.ncbi.nlm.nih.gov/pubmed/25759593
2) "The Yoga of Herbs," Dr David Frawley & Dr. Vasant Lad, p. 100

Apples
1) http://www.whfoods.com/genpage.php?tname=foodspice&dbid=15
2) http://www.ncbi.nlm.nih.gov/pubmed/20064576
3) http://www.ncbi.nlm.nih.gov/pubmed/22190137

Ashwagandha Root
1) http://www.mapi.com/ayurvedic-knowledge/amrit/benefits-of-an-ayurvedic-rasayana.html#gsc.tab=0
2) "The Way of Ayurvedic Herbs," Karta Purkh Singh Khalsa & Michael Tierra, p. 98
3) http://www.ncbi.nlm.nih.gov/pubmed/26068424

Astragalus
1) http://www.ncbi.nlm.nih.gov/pubmed/15015443
2) http://www.ncbi.nlm.nih.gov/pubmed/21426483

Avocado
1) http://archaeology.about.com/od/aterms/a/Avocado.htm
2) https://books.google.com/books?id=qwbhnqOYS_MC&pg=PA219&lpg=PA219&dq=oleic+acid
+myelin&source=bl&ots=CHY4Zjpll6&sig=11UDM4HBN6BlcYlm7iv_UvnRrP8&hl=en&sa=X&ved=0CFcQ6AEwB2oVChMIuYrF88utyAIVAiulCh2
Z0wUp#v=onepage&q=oleic%20acid%20myelin&f=false

Beef/Bison
1) http://journals.plos.org/plosone/article?id=10.1371/journal.pone.0046414
2) http://www.nutritionj.com/content/9/1/10
3) http://doctordavidcontreras.com/en/terapia.html

Beet Root
1) http://www.ergo-log.com/boron.html
2) http://draxe.com/what-is-betaine/
3) http://www.drdavidwilliams.com/importance-of-bile-acid/
4) "Anti-Aging Manual," Joseph B. Marion, pp. 297-298

lueberries
1) http://www.ncbi.nlm.nih.gov/pubmed/22111516
2) http://www.orac-info-portal.de/download/ORAC_R2.pdf

Broccoli
1) http://www.ncbi.nlm.nih.gov/pubmed/24466240

Cacao Bean
1) http://www.smithsonianmag.com/arts-culture/a-brief-history-of-chocolate-21860917/?no-ist
2) http://pubs.acs.org/doi/abs/10.1021/jf00011a009

Candy Caps
1) http://chromatographytoday.com/news/gc-mdgc-gc-ms/32/breaking_news/why_do_candy_cap_mushrooms_taste_like_maple_syrup/32363/

Carrot Root
1) "Healing with Whole Foods," Paul Pitchford, pp. 538-539
2) http://www.greenmedinfo.com/article/carrot-extract-protects-liver-chemical-injury

Cashews
1) http://www.mensjournal.com/health-fitness/nutrition/the-case-for-cashews-20140305

Cauliflower
1) https://www.pcrm.org/health/cancer-resources/diet-cancer/nutrition/how-isothiocyanates-help-protect-against-cancer

Celery
1) http://www.nytimes.com/1992/06/09/health/a-new-look-at-an-ancient-remedy-celery.html

Chaga Mushroom
1) http://www.faim.org/longevity/PPNF-Journal-Chaga.pdf
2) http://www.chagatrade.ru/pdfdocs/psoriasis_chaga.pdf
3) http://www.ncbi.nlm.nih.gov/pmc/articles/PMC2658785/

Chanca Piedra
1) http://docsdrive.com/pdfs/medwelljournals/ijmmas/2006/184-189.pdf
2) http://www.ncbi.nlm.nih.gov/pubmed/12010223
3) http://www.ncbi.nlm.nih.gov/pubmed/12599017

Chicken
1) "Food Energetics," Steve Gagne, p.163

Coconut Oil
1) http://online.liebertpub.com/doi/abs/10.1089/act.2006.12.310?src=recsys&journalCode=act
2) http://www.ncbi.nlm.nih.gov/pubmed/17651080

Coffee
1) http://onlinelibrary.wiley.com/doi/10.1111/j.1467-3010.2007.00665.x/full
2) http://content.iospress.com/articles/journal-of-alzheimers-disease/jad01404
3) http://www.scielo.org.co/scielo.php?pid=S0120-548X2012000100003&script=sci_arttext
4) http://www.scielo.br/scielo.php?pid=S1517-83822013000200006&script=sci_arttext
5) http://www.sciencedirect.com/science/article/pii/S0956713508002818

Collagen
1) http://bionumbers.hms.harvard.edu/bionumber.aspx?id=109730
2) "Anti-Aging Manual," Joseph B. Marion, p. 190

Colostrum
1) "Anti-Aging Manual," Joseph B Marion, p. 334
2) http://www.dravard.com/colostrum.htm

Crickets
1) http://www.pbs.org/newshour/rundown/bugs-for-dinner/
2) http://www.fao.org/docrep/018/i3253e/i3253e.pdf

Dragon Fruit
1) http://www.ncbi.nlm.nih.gov/pubmed/21434853
2) http://www.sciencedirect.com/science/article/pii/S0308814609013181

Eggs
1) http://www.1800chemist.com/p/The_Cholesterol_Controversy.pdf

Garlic
1) http://www.ncbi.nlm.nih.gov/pubmed/11238795
2) "The Yoga of Herbs," Dr. David Frawley & Dr. Vasant Lad, pp. 119-120
3) "The Art of Smart Thinking," James Hardt, PhD, pp. 81-84
4) http://www.ncbi.nlm.nih.gov/pubmed/15380627
5) http://www.ncbi.nlm.nih.gov/pubmed/15087243

Ghee
1) http://aem.asm.org/content/66/4/1654.abstract
2) http://lifespa.com/top-ten-reasons-cleanse-ghee/

Ginger Root
1) http://umm.edu/health/medical/altmed/herb/ginger
2) http://www.ncbi.nlm.nih.gov/pubmed/25230520
3) http://www.ncbi.nlm.nih.gov/pubmed/26355461
4) http://www.naturalnews.com/052009_ginger_chemotherapy_cancer_treatment.html

Goji Berry
1) http://www.ncbi.nlm.nih.gov/pubmed/21077258
2) http://www.ncbi.nlm.nih.gov/pubmed/24299844
3) http://www.ncbi.nlm.nih.gov/pubmed/24530338
4) http://www.ncbi.nlm.nih.gov/pubmed/24680899

Gynostemma
1) http://www.ncbi.nlm.nih.gov/pubmed/25371572
2) http://www.ncbi.nlm.nih.gov/pubmed/25066072
3) http://www.ncbi.nlm.nih.gov/pubmed/25066072

Jungle Peanuts
1) http://www.jacionline.org/article/S0091-6749(10)00575-0/abstract

Lecithin
1) http://dictionary.reference.com/browse/lecithin

Lion's Mane Mushroom
1) http://www.huffingtonpost.com/paul-stamets/mushroom-memory_b_1725583.html
2) ibid
3) http://www.ncbi.nlm.nih.gov/pubmed/26244378

Maca Powder
1) "The Healing Power of Rainforest Herbs," Leslie Taylor, ND, p. 339
2) http://onlinelibrary.wiley.com/doi/10.1111/j.1755-5949.2008.00052.x/full
3) http://www.maksfarma.com/Files/Maca/lepidium%20meyeni%28maca%29improved%20semen%20parameters.pdf

Mucuna Pruriens
1) http://www.academicjournals.org/journal/JMPR/article-abstract/63031A042671
2) http://www.ncbi.nlm.nih.gov/pubmed/18973898

Pearl Powder
1) http://www.justaboutskin.com/collagen-elastin-glycosasminoglycans/
2) "The Ancient Wisdom of the Chinese Tonic Herbs," Ron Teeguarden, pp. 175-176

Pomegrante
1) http://www.israel21c.org/top-10-great-reasons-to-love-the-pomegranate/
2) http://www.ncbi.nlm.nih.gov/pubmed/20043077
3) http://www.ncbi.nlm.nih.gov/pubmed/24949028

Probiotics
1) http://www.ncbi.nlm.nih.gov/pmc/articles/PMC2699871/
2) http://www.ncbi.nlm.nih.gov/pubmed/21876150

Psyllium Husk
1) http://umm.edu/health/medical/altmed/supplement/psyllium

Pumpkin Seed
1) http://www.ncbi.nlm.nih.gov/pubmed/22910218
2) http://www.ncbi.nlm.nih.gov/pubmed/16822218

Quinoa
1) "Food Energetics," Steve Gagne, p. 299
2) http://www.whfoods.com/genpage.php?tname=foodspice&dbid=142

Reishi Mushroom
1) http://onlinelibrary.wiley.com/doi/10.1002/ptr.830/abstract

Rice
1) http://www.mapi.com/ayurvedic-knowledge/plants-spices-and-oils/cook-ayurvedically-with-basmati-rice.html#gsc.tab=0
2) http://www.ncbi.nlm.nih.gov/pmc/articles/PMC1082903/
3) http://lifespa.com/whats-so-amazing-about-khichadi/

Salt
1) http://www.drkaslow.com/html/adrenal_insufficiency.html

Sesame Seeds
1) http://www.chineseherbshealing.com/black-sesame-seeds/
2) http://www.ncbi.nlm.nih.gov/pubmed/11588904

Sodium Copper Chlorophyllin
1) http://lpi.oregonstate.edu/mic/dietary-factors/phytochemicals/chlorophyll-chlorophyllin
2) http://www.ncbi.nlm.nih.gov/pubmed/25306371

Strawberry
1) http://www.sciencedirect.com/science/article/pii/S002364380500229X
2) http://www.naturalnews.com/046044_mercury_in_fish_strawberries_peanut_butter.html

Sweet Potato
1) http://www.all-about-sweet-potatoes.com/history-origin-sweet-potato.html
2) "Healing with Whole Foods," Paul Pitchford, p. 550
3) http://www.ncbi.nlm.nih.gov/pubmed/17645559

Tomato
1) "Healing with Whole Foods," Paul Pitchford, p. 544
2) https://www.google.com/patents/US6623769
3) http://www.ncbi.nlm.nih.gov/pubmed/17049831

Turmeric
1) http://www.ncbi.nlm.nih.gov/pubmed/9619120

Vanilla
1) http://www.ncbi.nlm.nih.gov/pubmed/25595338
2) NF-kB http://www.ncbi.nlm.nih.gov/pubmed/21250779

Walnuts
1) http://www.biolreprod.org/content/early/2012/08/07/biolreprod.112.101634.long
2) "Healing with Whole Foods," Paul Pitchford, p. 534
3) http://www.ncbi.nlm.nih.gov/pubmed/15979282

Water
1) https://en.wikipedia.org/wiki/Water_chlorination
2) http://www.fluorideresearch.org/343/files/FJ2001_v34_n3_p165-173.pdf
3) http://www2.cambridgema.gov/CityOfCambridge_Content/documents/140728%20jelstrup_1.PDF
4) http://www.foxnews.com/health/2013/12/18/is-your-drinking-water-on-drugs/
5) http://www.washingtonpost.com/wp-dyn/content/story/2008/03/09/ST2008030901877.html
6) http://journals.plos.org/plosone/article?id=10.1371/journal.pone.0055387

Whey Protein
1) http://www.ncbi.nlm.nih.gov/pmc/articles/PMC3821656/
2) http://www.ncbi.nlm.nih.gov/pubmed/1782728
3) http://www.ncbi.nlm.nih.gov/pubmed/12036812

Sweeteners of Choice

Honey
1) http://www.smithsonianmag.com/science-nature/the-science-behind-honeys-eternal-shelf-life-1218690/?no-ist
2) http://www.ncbi.nlm.nih.gov/pubmed/26101083
3) http://www.smithsonianmag.com/science-nature/the-science-behind-honeys-eternal-shelf-life-1218690/?no-ist
4) http://www.ncbi.nlm.nih.gov/pubmed/15117561

Lo Han Guo
1) http://www.itmonline.org/arts/luohanguo.htm
2) ibid

Stevia Leaf
1) "The Healing Power of Rainforest Herbs," Leslie Taylor, pp. 424-428

SugaVida
1) http://nopr.niscair.res.in/handle/123456789/22185
2) http://www.wseas.org/multimedia/journals/economics/2015/a205707-298.pdf
3) http://www.ncbi.nlm.nih.gov/pubmed/2000824
4) http://www.academicjournals.org/journal/JMPR/article-full-text-pdf/22525D714678

Birch Xylitol
1) "Applied BioChemistry and Biotechnology" 1997, Humana Press edited by Brian H. Davison, Mark Finkelstein, Charles E. Wyman, p. 118
2) "Xylitol inhibits carcinogenic acetaldehyde production by Candida species" Int J Cancer. 2011 Oct 15;129(8):2038-41. doi: 10.1002/ijc. 25844. Epub 2011 Apr 1.
3) http://www.ncbi.nlm.nih.gov/pubmed/14700079

Evolved Eating
1) http://discovermagazine.com/2013/may/13-grandmas-experiences-leave-epigenetic-mark-on-your-genes

The Game Changed
1) http://www.ewg.org/news/videos/10-americans,
2) http://www.worldometers.info/view/toxchem/
3) ibid
4) http://www.panna.org/blog/long-last-epa-releases-pesticide-use-statistics
5) http://www.ncbi.nlm.nih.gov/pmc/articles/PMC2946087/#R1
6) http://www.whatsonmyfood.org/level.jsp?food=IA&pesticide=B80
7) http://www.ncbi.nlm.nih.gov/pmc/articles/PMC1241915/
8) http://news.berkeley.edu/2010/03/01/frogs/
9) http://www.scientificamerican.com/article/common-herbicide-turns-male-frogs-into-females/
10) http://www.ncbi.nlm.nih.gov/pmc/articles/PMC3548883/
11) http://www.scielo.cl/pdf/jsspn/v15n1/aop0415.pdf
12) http://www.ncbi.nlm.nih.gov/pmc/articles/PMC4141693/
13) http://www.nytimes.com/2004/11/23/opinion/food-without-fear.html
14) http://www.mineralresourcesint.co.uk/pdf/mineral_deplet.pdf
15) http://www.scientificamerican.com/article/soil-depletion-and-nutrition-loss/
16) http://www.usgs.gov/newsroom/article.asp?ID=3919#.Vj5trXt98TM
17) http://www.bloomberg.com/bw/lifestyle/content/jun2010/bw20100622_903604.htm

Power of Powders

Blue Majik
1) http://www.sciencedirect.com/science/article/pii/S0006291X00937252
2) http://www.valensa.com/images3/Phycocyanin_The%20Wonder%20Molecule.pdf

Brain On
1) http://www.naturodoc.com/library/antiaging/PEA_science.htm

Pure Radiance
1) http://www.ncbi.nlm.nih.gov/pmc/articles/PMC3145266/

Eat, Drink & Glow!

"Rasa has at least two dozen important meanings in Sanskrit... the fact that Rasa means "taste" suggests that good Rasa Dhatu can be produced only when the ingested food possesses all the Tastes that the organism requires...

Rasa Dhatu's special function is "prinana," a word that means nourishment but is derived from a root that signifies romantic love. All bodies live from meal to meal, eternally craving further food. When the body is hungry, each of its cells is hungry. Just as a plant who is withering from lack of attention and water seems to freshen immediately when sprinkled by a thoughtful passerby, so too all of your cells perk up, physically and emotionally, when they receive the "sap" of Rasa Dhatu. Rasa is not sufficient in itself to nourish the whole organism, but it is a promise of better things to come.

Romance is an ephemeral emotion, which projects a potential to provide more. We feel great satisfaction from a glass of juice at the end of a long fast, and great relief from a glass of water after several hours of thirst. But those reactions are really just anticipations of the nourishment your tissues will experience after your digestion operates on that food or water. "Prinana" is the satisfaction you feel when the nourishment first enters your system.

It is called "romantic love" because it is really a waltz of two separate existences – you and the food – who are trying to become sufficiently intimate with one another to unite together. The sense of danger, the exaltation of excitement, the thrill of the unknown and all the other emotions including the lust your feel when you fall in love you also feel, in simpler form, when your body is suffused with the fresh Rasa from a well-digested meal."

- DR. ROBERT E. SVOBODA, from "PRAKRITI"

Index

C

D

E

F

G

M

Q

T

U

V

W